*STORIES FROM*

# JEWISH PORTLAND

# STORIES FROM JEWISH PORTLAND

Polina Olsen

THE History PRESS

Published by The History Press
Charleston, SC 29403
www.historypress.net



First published 2011

Manufactured in the United States

ISBN 978.1.60949.348.6

Library of Congress Cataloging-in-Publication Data

Olsen, Polina.
Stories from Jewish Portland / Polina Olsen.
p. cm.
Includes bibliographical references and index.
ISBN 978-1-60949-348-6
1. Jews--Oregon--Portland--History. 2. Portland (Or.)--Ethnic relations. I. Title.
F884.P89J54 2011
305.89240795'49--dc23
2011019205

*For Andy.*

# CONTENTS

# Contents

# FOREWORD

The *Jewish Review* has called on the writing talent of Polina Olsen for a number of years, asking her to cover events or write profiles as a freelance writer. During those years, the newspaper also publicized the walks that Polina periodically led around the former Jewish community of Old South Portland. In 2009, we finally had the good sense to combine her talents for writing, interviewing and historic research. When we received a grant to support adding new content to the *Jewish Review*, we asked Polina to become a contributing editor of the newspaper and write a "Looking Back" column.

The first "Looking Back" ran in the *Jewish Review* on February 15, 2009, and was headlined "Old South Portlanders Kibbitz After All These Years."

Elderly readers began calling in with their own memories and ideas for stories. And newcomers e-mailed to say that they had had no idea of their new home's history. Polina's historical tidbits and insights fit in well with the *Jewish Review*'s mission to help build and strengthen community. Polina's columns have made a nice addition to the *Jewish Review*, providing a diversity to our pages previously unavailable.

When the Jewish Federation of Greater Portland began its celebration of ninety years of serving the community, we again turned to Polina for historical perspective. Through diligent research and interviews, she once more provided a picture of an evolving community in a series of articles that stretched from the federation's roots to the present.

Her stories seem to touch a chord with young and old alike, awakening awareness in some and memories in others.

Deborah Moon
City Editor, *Jewish Review*
6680 Southwest Capitol Highway
Portland, Oregon 97219

# ACKNOWLEDGEMENTS

My first thanks go to Paul Haist and Deborah Moon of the *Jewish Review* for the opportunity to research and write about Oregon's Jewish community. I'd also like to thank my commissioning editor Aubrie Koenig at The History Press for her interest, suggestions and encouragement.

I've benefited from the help of many people, including Evelyn Banko; Frank Barnett; Edie Nudelman Bean; Francis Riback Berger; Norman Berlant; Elizabeth Blane; Marc Blattner; Henry Blauer; Randy Blazak; Vivienne Bonnin; Bonnie Boren; Deborah Reinhardt Brandt; Elie Bulka; Milt Carl; Esther Chernichowsky; Carol Chestler; Frieda Cohen; Hazel Dakers; Gary Dielman and Perry Stokes of the Baker County Library; Ike Donin; Dorothy Dworkin; the late Marvin (Mutzy) Enkelis; Marcia Ketzlach Gale; Dr. John Gevurtz; Raya Lippman Gladstein; Harry Glickman; Anita Gold; Jane Goldhamer; Vera Goldman; the late Leo Greenstein; Marilyn Krane Hasson; Milt Hasson; John and Judy Hisenteger of the Portland Interscholastic League Hall of Fame; Hy Jackson; Carol Jaffee; the Jewish Genealogical Society of Oregon; Leatrice Kaplan; Dr. Nancy Korloff; Priscilla Kostiner; Ann Kruss; Dr. Daniel Labby; Ruth Lindemann; Louise Lorente; Stan and Susan Marcus; Toinette Menashe; James Meyer; Harold Mink; Rabbi Chaim Mishulovin; Simi Mishulovin; Bryna Montgomery; Allison Mudrick; Dr. Larry Mudrick; Raisa Premysler; Shirley Rackner; the late Gussie Reinhardt; Flora Rigotti; Laurie Rogoway; the late Jack Rosen; Norman, Judy and Jay Rosenbloom; Elden Rosenthal; Todd

Rosenthal; Becka Ross; Kyle Rotenberg; the late Irving Rotenberg; Carol Schubach Salasky; the late Harold Saltzman; Ruth Saltzman; Jack Sanders; Charlie Schiffman; Rob Schlacter; Charlotte Schwartz; Carolyn Shain; Elinor Shank; Arden Shenker; Rita and Mark Shmulevsky; Linda Singer; Eloise Durkheimer Spiegel; Josh Stein; Morris Stein; Jerry Stern; Vicki Stone; Chuck Tauman; John Trachtenberg; Jim Turner; the late Harry Turtledove; Ken Unkeles; Nina Weinstein; the late Lillian Wexler; Devorah Wilhelm; Rabbi Moshe Wilhelm; Rabbi Motti Wilhelm; and Francis Aiken Wolfe. Finally, I would like to thank my wonderful husband, Andy, and my mother, Mrs. Lillian Lionel, for their unending support.

*Introduction*

# A Short History of Jewish Oregon

Fables from the old Wild West don't usually include Jewish businessmen. Still, from Pendleton to North Powder, Heppner, Burns and Browntown, it was German Jewish immigrants minding the store. Their history in Oregon dates to the 1848 California gold rush. They followed prospectors as peddlers or general store owners and moved north as new deposits were found.

During the 1850s, Jewish communities developed in three Oregon cities. Jacob Goldstein and Lewis May arrived in Portland in 1849. One year after the 1851 Jacksonville gold discovery, seven Jews lived among the 1,506 residents. Jacob and Louis Fleischner arrived in Albany via the Oregon Trail in 1852.

Most early Jews immigrated to the United States from Germany. They integrated into the larger community and formed Jewish institutions. Jacksonville's High Holiday services started in 1856 and the Jewish cemetery in 1859. Jews worked on the Jacksonville City Council, and Max Muller was postmaster for eighteen years.

As in Jacksonville, Albany's Jewish residents soon dominated businesses along the main street. They ran dry goods, groceries and clothing stores, a barbershop, a saloon and even a ladies' hairdressing salon. Albert Senders owned a grain mill, served as town mayor and became exalted ruler of the Elks Lodge. Prussian immigrant Julius Joseph joined the Seventeenth Missouri Volunteer Infantry during the Civil War before moving to Albany and opening a tobacco store.

Front Avenue in downtown Portland, 1910. *Courtesy City of Portland Archives, Oregon, View of Front Ave., AP/7080, 1910.*

The First Hebrew Congregation of Albany was formed in 1878, primarily to organize a cemetery. Burials also brought Portland Jews together. The Mount Sinai Burial Association formed in 1856 with land in what coincidentally became the Jewish and Italian immigrant district of South Portland. Congregation Beth Israel absorbed the association when they organized in 1858.

Simon and Jacob Blumauer opened their shop on Portland's Front Avenue in 1851, the year the city incorporated. Aaron Meier peddled in the Oregon Territory before opening his store in 1857. By 1860, 120 Jews lived in Portland out of a population of 2,874.

Jews followed gold and livestock to small towns. Samuel Marks and Hyman Wolenberg purchased Canyonville in 1863. Bavarian brothers Sigmund and Seligmann Heilner's long history in Oregon started with Seligmann's 1845 immigration. He opened a dry goods store in Crescent City, California. Sigmund joined him but soon headed north to Browntown, a small mining settlement over the Oregon border. A February 15, 1865 *Morning Oregonian* article titled "A Trip through Josephine County" recorded those times:

> *We next paid a visit to the mill and mine belonging to S.A. Heilner, Esquire, located near Democrat Gulch. This lode is situated on the mountain, about*

Sigmund A. Heilner, 1837–1917. *Courtesy Baker County (Oregon) Library Historic Photo Collection.*

> *one and a half miles from the mill, having an excellent wagon road constructed between the two points. At the suggestion of Mr. Heilner, we, in company with our friend Evans, each bearing a candle in hand, commenced the ascent of the shaft, not knowing the magnitude of the undertaking, but supposing that a few feet would bring us to the top. Water came down like a torrent of rain; Ominous thought passed through our minds…But, at length a light gleamed from above, and looking up, we saw Mr. Heilner holding a candle.*

Near Grants Pass, Asher and Solomon Marks owned a sawmill and flume on Mule Creek. The Rogue River Ranch National Historic Site preserves remnants of Marial, the tiny nearby town. Near Glendale, Russian Jews founded the New Odessa agricultural commune on land they had bought from Canyonville settler, Hyman Wolenberg. They created their community for "mutual assistance in perfecting and development of physical, mental, and moral capacities of its members," according to the articles of incorporation.

With the 1861 discovery of gold near Baker County, Jews fanned out to eastern Oregon. A June 4, 1873 *Morning Oregonian* article referred to

After gold was discovered in Baker County, many Jewish families made the journey to eastern Oregon. This photograph shows the Heilner brothers' store. Remnants of it are all that remain of Sparta. *Courtesy Baker County (Oregon) Library Historic Photo Collection.*

brothers Sigmund and Seligmann Heilner, formerly of Crescent City and Browntown: "In Sparta, Union County, there are two stores, one hotel, two saloons and two blacksmith shops. There are several families there. Coan Bros. are putting up a fine stone building." Seligmann Heilner went by the alias E.D. Cohen to avoid creditors, which apparently confused the reporter. Today, the brother's store is all that remains of the old mining town.

Eventually, the Heilner brothers moved to Baker City. Here, Seligmann was shot dead outside his brother's store while serving as a court case witness. Sigmund married Clara Neuberger and had four children. Their son, Richard Neuberger, became Oregon's second Jewish United States senator.

The Leo Adler House Museum demonstrates the legacy of another Jewish Baker City family. Carl Adler owned the Crystal Palace, a general merchandise store. Known as "Mr. Baker," his son, Leo, made a fortune in the magazine distribution business and left $20 million to the town.

Eloise Durkheimer Spiegel remembered her grandfather's stories about Burns, a small town that served sheep and cattle ranchers. He owned the general store and doubled as town mayor. "He closed the store for Rosh Hashanah, but the Indians didn't understand that it was temporarily," she said. "There was some kind of uprising, so when Yom Kippur came he closed it again but had someone standing guard."

Jack Sanders, a retired University of Oregon professor, is an authority on Pendleton's Jewish community and author of *Samuel Rothchild: A Jewish Pioneer in the Days of the Old West*. "Although there is little evidence of Jewish culture in Pendleton, Oregon, today, members of this merchant class were critical to the development," he said in a telephone interview. Sanders learned that a Jewish congregation formed in 1879. "There was no ordained rabbi, and the congregation elected businessman Lehman Blum. One general store, L. Dusenbery & Co., closed for Rosh Hashanah and Yom Kippur. These closings were announced in the *East Oregonian*, although the *EO* spellings are a cause of amusement."

Meanwhile, in 1885, Samuel Rothchild's cousin, Herman, moved to North Powder. When he died in 1924, the *North Powder News* called him the city's most prominent man:

> *Last Saturday evening about fifty or more North Powder people motored to Baker to pay their last respects to the old merchant. These were members of the I.O.O.F. and Rebekah lodges of this city, the city council, and businessmen of the town. When the remains were taken from West's chapel to the depot, the North Powder people followed in their cars, to show their keen respect for North Powder's most prominent man. Many who wished to honor Mr. Rothchild, but could not go to Baker, assembled at the North Powder depot, and as the train slowed down to four miles an hour, raised their hats and bowed in respect. The railroad company consented to running No. 18 at four miles an hour through this city at the request of George T. Ballard, station agent.*
>
> *In the years gone by Herman Rothchild was the most prominent and influential citizen of North Powder. He served as its first mayor and was re-elected to a second term. He refused to accept the office a third time. He also served as city treasurer and was a member of the school board. He for many years conducted a successful mercantile business with H.O. Gorham, afterwards taking over the business. He has done more for the people of this city and rural districts than any other individual. Through*

> *the period of hard times he extended credit to everybody and anybody, a hazardous venture, and survived, though many others less lenient failed. For this reason, he must be given great credit for the development of the town and country adjacent to North Powder.*
>
> *No citizen of North Powder ever enjoyed the popularity and acquaintance over the state as did Mr. Rothchild. In 1906 he was elected to the state legislature, the only democrat to succeed for the place in the entire state. At that term of legislature he was also the only Hebrew in its body, and the combination of being the only democrat and only Hebrew in the state legislature brought a great deal of comment from the state press. Being witty, Mr. Rothchild in a humorous speech, nominated himself as speaker of the house, saying he had the support of every democrat and Jew in the house. Mr. Davey, of Salem, who was elected speaker, gave Mr. Rothchild a complimentary vote for the place.*

Meanwhile, throughout the United States established Jews encouraged new immigrants to become farmers. The Hebrew Agricultural Association of Oregon was incorporated in 1912. First year officers included A. Zidell, president, and Rabbi Jonah B. Wise, first vice-president. "The object of this organization is to be the encouragement of agriculture among the Jews," noted a July 5 *Jewish Tribune* article. "This organization will lend money without interest and otherwise assist Jewish farmers in their vocation."

By August, the *Jewish Tribune* reported, "Twenty-five Jewish families, including a shochet, will leave Sunday to file on government lands in Central Oregon." The group settled in the high desert of Lake County, near the town of Paisley. The *Lake City Examiner* picked up the story in an October 3, 1912 article titled "Colonization in Northern Lake":

> *Of vast importance to the early development of the upper part of the Lake County is the settlement of a Hebrew colony near Rams Rock. Mr. Schatter* [sic] *who was acting as spokesman for the party informed the Examiner that 25 families would follow this fall. All the land was taken under the three year Homestead Act and this year they expect to get contracts for clearing land and getting it under cultivation.*

Scattered reports continued over the next few years. A January 1, 1914 *Morning Oregonian* article under the headline "Jews Form Oregon Colony" reported:

> *Of the entire colony, only 15 families remain, the others having scattered to take up residence in and around Bend. The families that constitute the colony in the "Jewish Valley," as it is now known, are satisfied with what they have done the first year…This is the beginning of Jewish colonization on public lands in Oregon.*

Despite the initial success, Jewish farmers—along with most others in the area—found the land unsuitable for cultivation. David Pearlman and Jacob Mayers stayed long enough to receive land patents. Within a few years, the only thing left of this Jewish colony in Lake County was the place name "Jew Valley," which is still listed in *Oregon Geographic Names*.

## Portland's Early Jews

Mining declined. Railroad expansion and lower shipping costs brought increased competition to the established merchants. Settlers worried about their children's Jewish education. Most Jews left small towns for Portland.

In Portland, Jews lived near their downtown businesses at first but eventually moved toward the Park Blocks and the Northwest. Several were among the city's most prominent citizens. Louis Fleischner left his brother in Albany and fought in the Rogue River Indian War. The Portland dry goods store that he opened in 1864 became a leading wholesale house. The city purchased Washington Park during Bernard Goldsmith's 1869–72 term as mayor. Joseph Simon was state senator from 1880 to 1891 and was mayor in 1909. The cast-iron façade of the building named for him still stands on Northwest Third Avenue.

Multnomah County sheriff Benjamin L. Norden served from 1878 to 1880. According to his descendant, Hazel Dakers, Norden's family were among the earliest practicing Jews of South Africa. After his father's death in the South African Frontier War, Benjamin and his mother settled in Portland. The following letter, which appeared in the August 21, 1861 *Weekly*

Isaac and Cacelie Gevurtz at the beach. Isaac Gevurtz (1850–1917) emigrated from Poznan, Poland, and owned a downtown furniture store. *Courtesy Dr. John Gevurtz.*

*Oregonian*, shows Norden as secretary to Congregation Beth Israel when they built their first synagogue:

> *At a special meeting of the Congregation of Beth-Israel of this city, held last evening in the Vestry Room of their new Synagogue, the following resolution was adopted:*
>
> *Resolved, that the sincere thanks of this congregation are eminently due and are here by respectfully tendered to their friends and fellow citizens, for their generous assistance towards the erection of their new Synagogue, which was duly consecrated on this day.*
>
> *Benjamin L. Norden, Sec'y.*
> *Portland, August 15, 1861.*

Norden also worked as a fire officer and as secretary to the Sportsman's Club before becoming sheriff. Newspaper articles, like this February 8, 1879 *Morning Oregonian* story, gave grisly accounts of his tenure:

> *James Cook was executed here to-day at 1 o'clock. He ate a hearty breakfast this morning and talked freely to everybody that came in to see him. He slept well last night, and acted like a boy let loose from a long term of school. A guard of ten armed men was posted around the jail at 12:30. Father Gauden, the Catholic priest, went to Cook's cell at 12:35 and remained there…until they walked to the scaffold…* [Sheriff] *Crossen told him to stop on the trap, which he did and his ankles were strapped. Cook then took leave of Sheriff Crossen, Father Gauden, Sheriffs Norden and Schuster and Deputy Sheriff Haines.*

Ben Norden married Irish immigrant Mary Maher and had three children. The February 11, 1898 *Morning Oregonian* announced his early death under the headline "Prominent in Local Politics for Thirty Years." A February 14 article reported that the worthy master of the Harmony Lodge conducted the funeral: "The remarkable feature…was the presence of so many older citizens of Portland—men who have lived in the city half a century or more…The body was conveyed to Riverview cemetery for internment where the final services by the Masonic order were conducted."

Another newspaper published in Portland recorded life in those early times. The *American Hebrew News* (1893–1901) blared headlines like "The Woman's Exchange Is Arranging a Grand Ball at the Marquam." The Oregon Cracker Company advertised "Matzos! Matzos! Matzos!" while other stores offered "Ham—Great Reductions in Prices." Notices about Seaside and Gearhart resorts started in about 1897. Reports on B'nai B'rith lodges reflected Portland's increasingly stratified society.

In the early 1900s, Eastern European and Sephardic Jews settled in South Portland. They built a self-contained community with kosher butcher shops, bakeries and synagogues that reflected their religious orthodoxy. They organized a free-loan and burial society and started small businesses. Many became junk peddlers.

Hundreds of Eastern European Jews came to Oregon under the auspices of the Industrial Removal Office (IRO). The IRO relocated Jewish workers from New York's Lower East Side to Jewish communities throughout the country. It hoped that dispersion would ease slum conditions and prevent anti-immigrant legislation. Ben Selling became Portland's IRO representative.

*Left*: The bima of Kesser Israel Synagogue on Southwest Meade Street. *Courtesy Elie Bulka, Oolite Photography.*

*Below*: Hyman Kirshner (back left) founded the Modish Coat and Suit Company in 1923. It became one of the largest manufacturing shops of its kind on the West Coast. *Courtesy Anita Gold.*

With the help of the Hebrew Benevolent Association, he located work and housing and notified the New York headquarters.

Although cultural differences continued until the next generation, German Jews like Selling helped the newcomers. The National Council of Jewish Women founded Neighborhood House, a community center in the heart of the immigrant district. It offered athletics, a kindergarten, a dispensary, citizenship classes and a Hebrew school on the top floor. Ida Loewenberg, whose Prussian-born father made and then lost a fortune, directed the center for thirty-two years. Her sister, Zerlina, became the neighborhood librarian.

Women's suffrage became a burning issue throughout Portland. In 1912, Oregon women won the right to vote after six unsuccessful campaigns dating back to 1884. As elsewhere in society, Jews had mixed reactions. The *Jewish Tribune*, which was published in Portland between 1903 and 1919, carried antisuffrage editorials during 1912. "We are against woman suffrage for the good of the women themselves and for the good of our country," the editor

Portland businessman and philanthropist Jerry Stern attended kindergarten in 1931 at the Neighborhood House. In this photo, he is the last boy seated in the center row. *Courtesy Jerry Stern.*

wrote. Although the Council of Jewish Women did not support suffrage at a national level, Portland Section ex-president and board member Josephine Hirsch founded the Portland Equal Suffrage League. PESL archives obtained from the Library of Congress include Neighborhood House notes like "increasing attendance at sewing school" and "attendance at bible classes larger than ever" scribbled across Oregon Equal Suffrage Association Letterhead.

By the 1920s, South Portland Jews had started moving to Laurelhurst and other east side neighborhoods. By this time, Portland's Jewish population numbered about 9,000 out of 275,000.

## THE HOLOCAUST AND ZIONISM

Frieda Cohen remembered hearing about the Holocaust in 1938. "Jewish leaders everywhere brought it to our attention," she said. "We were all outspoken, especially Rabbi Berkowitz of Temple Beth Israel. The community became tight, sticking together even more than before. My mother and aunt saved money to buy clothes and sent them to their family in Poland. We never heard from them."

Zionism was important to most of the Jewish community. The Portland Chapter of Hadassah, the largest Zionist organization, was started in 1920 under the leadership of Paula Lauterstein. After the Holocaust, a Jewish homeland took on additional urgency. The late Gussie Reinhardt remembered that night in 1947.

"I'll never forget it," she said in a 2005 interview. "The United Nations was voting. Would they partition Palestine and create a Jewish state? We stayed up all night listening to the radio. Once the UN voted *yes*, the new country needed a name. Leaders like David Ben-Gurion and Golda Meier chose Israel, which was perfect."

Meanwhile, the population grew. According to the 1957 Jewish Welfare Federation of Portland census, 7,832 Jews lived in Portland at that time. Almost half were born in Oregon; 26 percent were foreign born compared with 8 percent of the population as a whole, 68 percent belonged to a synagogue and nearly half were self-employed.

Portland Jews moved back to the west side but not to South Portland. A 1960s Urban Renewal project demolished much of the old neighborhood.

Molly Tushinsky Cohen, Kate Tushinsky Braunstein, Sarah Tushinsky Stern and Ida Tushinsky Holtzman at Kate's wedding in Portland, circa 1915. *Courtesy Ruth Saltzman.*

Young married couples liked the new Hillsdale suburbs, with modern houses, larger yards and nearby shopping malls. When Congregation Neveh Shalom was formed in 1961, Rabbi Stampfer and others felt that building on the east side would be "disastrous to the future of the congregation since the movement of the Jewish population was decidedly to the West Side but away from the downtown area," according to historian Gary Miranda.

The *Jewish Review* was started in 1959 as an arm of the Jewish Welfare Federation of Portland, now called the Jewish Federation of Greater Portland. International and local events that affected Oregon's Jews hit the paper's front page.

The newspaper and Jews everywhere focused during the 1967 Arab-Israeli War. Portlanders responded with record levels of donations. Other major issues followed, like the 1972 Soviet Jewry rally in Portland and the murder of Israeli athletes in Munich. The paper reflected how readers united over the fate of Russian Jews and any threat to Israel, as well as racism. When Portland attorney Elden Rosenthal assisted Morris Dees in convicting white supremacist Tom Metzger for his role in the 1988 murder of Ethiopian immigrant Mulugeta Seraw, it generated front-page news and a sense of collective pride.

Today, Jews are again scattered throughout Oregon, with synagogues from Klamath Falls to Bend. Jacksonville's community meets at its Jewish deli for Passover. Portland's Jewish population stands at 45,700.

Since the gold rush brought Jews to Oregon, they've fought in wars, helped build towns and served as mayors. They've contributed to museums, concert halls and shelters for the disadvantaged. They joined the larger community in business, government and philanthropy but never forgot their roots. As Steven Lowenstein said in his 1987 book *The Jews of Oregon*, "Perhaps it is this sense of self, of peoplehood, that has allowed Jews to reach out and participate so fully in the building of Oregon."

*Part I*

# AN IMMIGRATION STORY

Aaron Meier typified Portland's early Jewish settlers. Arriving from Bavaria in 1855, he clerked at his brother's dry goods store in the gold rush town of Downieville, California, before heading out to peddle in the Oregon territory. In 1857, he opened a general merchandising store on Front Avenue in Portland. By 1860, the city's population of 2,874 included 120 Jews.

Waves of immigrants followed the early German Jews. Before 1900, few Jews lived in the South Portland neighborhood, but by 1920 there were 6,000, according to author Steven Loewenstein. The area filled with Turkish and Greek Jews who had migrated from Seattle and with Eastern Europeans whose first stop was often New York City. The Industrial Removal Office, a concerted effort to move Jews out of New York, brought several hundred to Oregon. The great Portland philanthropist Ben Selling served as the local IRO contact.

During the 1940s, Holocaust survivors formed the Friendship Club at the Neighborhood House. Social service agencies, although stretched, helped them adjust to their new home. By the time Soviet Jews arrived in the 1970s and again in the 1990s, the Jewish Family and Child Service had well-organized teams.

This chapter tells the history of Jewish migration to Portland through the stories of people who lived through those times. Beginning with a girl whose uncle founded the small town of Heppner through to Russian resettlement,

*Left*: Jewish family in Russia. Rachel Holtzman, seated center with headscarf, is Portlander Ruth Saltzman and Arlene Schnitzer's great-grandmother. *Courtesy Ruth Saltzman.*

*Below*: Lubov Kazakova (left) and Vilen Oganyan at the Victory Day celebrations at the MJCC, 2010. *Photo by author.*

resilience, adaptability and gratitude to this country shine through loud and clear. Vera Goldman, who emigrated in 1990, summed it up in a 2010 interview: "We said bye-bye Russia because it's a place not for Jewish people. For the past twenty years, I've been an American."

## Early Jews Home on the Range

The California gold rush attracted thousands out west, including Jewish merchants. They opened general stores or peddled to miners and migrated north with the gold. They scattered throughout Oregon's small towns and often served as town mayors.

Mining declined and competition increased. Parents wanted a Jewish education for their children. Most left the small towns for Portland or other large cities. Today, only memories of growing up Jewish in frontier Oregon remain.

Hy Jackson grew up in Baker, where his father and uncle traveled into the countryside buying and selling wool and animal hides. "A farmer told my

In 1887, German Jewish immigrant Carl Adler opened the Crystal Palace in Baker, Oregon. *Courtesy Baker County (Oregon) Library Historic Photo Collection.*

father the men around Wallowa Lake were pretty wild," he said. "My dad went out, bought a gun and went practice shooting."

"My father was from the Vilna area," he continued. "My grandmother put acid in his ear so he wouldn't have to go into the Russian army. He came to America as quite a young man—about seventeen. He had two brothers out west. I have no idea how he got to Oregon."

Jackson's mother was among a group of Portland Jews that had migrated from Pueblo, Colorado. The couple met in Vale, Oregon, and settled in Baker City. Jackson has vivid memories of going out on the road with his uncle. He bought wool from farmers, hides from slaughterhouses or butchers and fur from trappers. "As they gathered these items together, they went to factories," Jackson said. "Wool went to woolen mills, furs to furriers, hides to tanners or brokers and cascara bark to pharmaceutical companies. We slept at little hotels. They were so bad, but when you closed your eyes, you were satisfied. Sometimes we stayed in a home. The food was magnificent.

Isador and Mose Fuchs were part of a Baker family Hy Jackson remembered. *Courtesy Baker County (Oregon) Library Historic Photo Collection.*

I never saw a bad spread. For breakfast, they had ham and eggs. For dinner, the meats were marvelous."

Several Jewish families lived in Baker. "There were the Heilners, Adlers, Levys and Fuchs," Jackson said. "Some practiced their Judaism and some not." His family always joined relatives in Portland for Jewish holidays. When it came time for him to study for his Bar Mitzvah, the family moved to Portland.

Francis Aiken Wolfe's family settled in Union, Oregon, a small town thirty-five miles north of Baker. The 1880 census shows her grandparents, Isaac and Sarah Bloch Boskowitz, with three children and a dry goods store. Originally from Bavaria, Isaac Boskowitz immigrated in about 1863. Sarah Bloch's parents were also German immigrants. They settled in Alabama but left for Oregon during the Civil War.

"I heard about Union all my life," Wolfe said. "The houses were old, and there was nothing pretentious about them. And they used an outhouse. As my mother said, on a cold winter day, there was nothing pleasant about it."

Francis Aiken Wolfe's family. *From left*: her grandmother, Sarah Boskowitz; her mother, Miriam (with muff); her aunt, Minnie; and her great-aunt, Sophie. *Courtesy Francis Aiken Wolfe.*

Wolfe never heard stories of anti-Semitism. Jews owned the town's two main stores. Although her mother attended Catholic school, the family celebrated Jewish holidays "as best they could in a small town." Her religiously observant great-grandmother also lived in Union and reportedly kept kosher.

"How she did this, I have no idea," Wolfe said. "Maybe they ate the forepart of the cow but didn't eat the back. My aunts [in Portland] bought only forequarter meat, and then they soaked it in salt. That was the best way they could keep it kosher."

Heppner, named after Henry Heppner, the German Jew who founded it, lies 125 miles west of Union. The town's population was under two hundred when Elinor Shank was growing up. "When gold was discovered in the John Day country and the interior of Idaho, Henry Heppner ran mule trains and carried supplies," Shank said. "In about 1872, he fell in love with the location of Heppner. He bought the interest of Mr. Morrow, for whom the county is named, and built a store."

Shank's father, born in Shasta, California, migrated to Heppner to work for his Uncle Henry. Shank remembered her childhood home. "You walked into a vestibule. There was a settee with a fur rug thrown over it of some unknown animal," she said. "The house had two large bedrooms and a sleeping porch. The kitchen had marvelous cabinetry, lovely wooden counters and a majestic cooking range. Beyond the kitchen, the keeping room had an ironing board, refrigerator and stairway to the cellar. The toilet was just opposite the back door—no washbowl, just a toilet."

The town had one restaurant owned by a Chinese couple but no African Americans, Shank said. "The Umatilla Reservation is near Heppner, and the Native-Americans did their trading there. I remember seeing them in my dad's store. They traded pelts for stock feed. During World War I, a man of German parentage ran a piano store. He had a hard time and finally left. It was sad."

Shank continued:

> *We had access to things like fresh pork sausage made by a neighbor. It was just pork with pepper and sage. The combination was wonderful. Beef tongue was a favorite in our family, along with chicken, pork roast, beef, and homemade bacon and ham. On Friday, the fish arrived. This was a strong*

*Catholic community. I remember halibut or salmon on Fridays and oysters at holidays. We celebrated Christmas with an exchange of gifts.*

*Kids played in the street. The only tennis court was on the school grounds. Of course, in the summer there was a lot of swimming. Three other girls and I had a little camp in the upper end of town at the bend of the creek. The father of one owned some property. We built a hut that began with blankets, tarps and 2x4s and finally got enough money to buy lumber. And there was a Chautauqua each year. It's a series of entertainment and educational programs. In those days, they sent performers out to towns and set up in a big tent, like a circus. The afternoons and evenings were geared to adults, but the mornings were for kids.*

Shank's father bought and sold wool and grain. During World War I, her mother became the county Red Cross chair. "She and two men were the speakers bureau, and they went into the interior to sell Liberty Bonds," Shank said. "When they got to the small town of Monument, the people didn't know there was a war going on."

Shank's family became the only Jews in town when the Blackman family left. "It was like being the only anything else," she said. "No discrimination, nothing detrimental. I knew my parents were Jewish, and I had a book of Old Testament Bible stories. At that time, that was the end of my [religious] education."

Still, when the family moved to Portland, they enrolled Shank at Temple Beth Israel's religious school. She became a kindergarten teacher at the Neighborhood House and married a Jewish man. "We lived in Coos Bay, and I had a religious school for the Jewish kids," she said. "My daughter was confirmed at Temple; my son was Bar Mitzvahed."

## Coming to America

Stories about the old country were about poverty and fighting for the czar. Maybe that's why few of our ancestors talked about where they grew up, why they left Europe and how they came to America. Painstaking genealogical research reveals a skeleton of their lives in shipping manifests or city directories. Only the people who remember can put flesh on the bones.

Dora and Jacob Schneiderman immigrated to South Portland from Russia. *Courtesy Jack Rosen.*

Leo Greenstein (1920–2011) shared his memories in a 2005 interview. His parents emigrated from Russia in the early 1900s and settled in South Portland.

"My dad's parents lived in a village with few Jews, so they sent him to a Beth Midrash," he said. "He slept there and ate at a different home every night." Greenstein's mother lived among relatives after her mother's early death. "She worked in a factory, I think making matches. They gave her a stool to stand on."

Greenstein's parents talked about life among Russians. "They said, as a whole, the Russian people weren't bad but awfully poor. The only time [my parents] had fear was around Easter and Christmas when the priest would harangue the people."

How did they come to America? "Ben Selling [Portland Jewish philanthropist] might have been the one who brought my parents over," Greenstein said. "The immigrants didn't know who was helping, they just knew someone was. My dad had to avoid the Russian draft so he had to sneak across the border, but fortunately there was graft. My mother had a sister in Portland, and when she came here she met my dad."

Greenstein's family settled on Southwest Gibbs Street. "It was a small one-story house with a dirt basement—nothing special about it," he said. "In the summertime my dad would sit out on the porch, and people would walk by, stop and come up. It was an entirely different kind of life. In some ways, it was very nice, but people were a lot poorer. Life was much harder."

Gussie Kirshner Reinhardt (1908–2005) was the grande dame of Portland's Jewish community. She grew up across the street from Kesser Israel Synagogue, of which her father was president for forty years. Like Leo Greenstein's father, Oscar Kirshner relied on graft to facilitate his escape from Russia, according to a 2006 interview with his granddaughter, Deborah Reinhardt Brandt.

Gussie Reinhardt was an iconic figure in Portland's Jewish community. This photo shows her parents, Anna and Oscar Kirshner, with sister Ora and brother Hymie. *Courtesy Deborah Reinhardt Brandt.*

"My grandfather played the coronet in the czar's army," Brandt said. "He made a pact with my grandmother that when his number came up to fight, he would escape. He left with four silver spoons to use as bribes and with his tefillin, which he wrapped around his head when he swam across a river. He went around the Black Sea and took a boat to America. He kept the spoons in the kitchen table drawer, and he took them out and counted them every day."

Like many immigrants, Kirshner came to America first and saved money to send for his family. "A couple years later, he sent for my grandmother," Brandt said. "My uncles, Isadore and Hymie, and my aunt, Ora, were born in Russia. They came over in steerage. Bubbe made important friends on the boat. They came to Portland, too."

The czar's army filled Jews with terror. Escaping conscription was a common reason for emigrating. Some parents cut off a son's finger or otherwise mutilated him to avoid the draft. Others, like Harry Turtledove's great-grandfather, spent twenty years in military service.

"He was an orthodox Jew," Turtledove (1921–2011) said in a 2005 interview. "I don't know how he survived." The czar rewarded him with permission to travel throughout Russia and live in Moscow, both ordinarily forbidden to Jews. He settled in Moscow, became a lumber merchant and, when the time came, sent his two sons to England to avoid the Russian draft.

In England, Turtledove's grandfather became a cabinetmaker. "The family story is the king's physician examined him and said he needed a dryer climate," Turtledove said. "He went to Oakland, California, which at that time was a car-building center for the railroad, so he got employment. My grandmother made wigs for Orthodox ladies to put bread on the table. Grandfather decided Oakland was too rough a place to bring up a good Jewish family, so escaping England for a dry climate, he came to Portland."

In Portland, Turtledove's grandfather opened a secondhand clothing store on Third and Burnside. His daughter, Turtledove's mother, who had remained in England, joined the family in 1912. "The shipping manifest says she was sixteen years old and a domestic," he said. "She never talked about it. People made a new life, and they closed the book."

## Archives of the Industrial Removal Office Reveal Forgotten History

*Nov 24, 1905*
*274 Sheridan St.*
*Portland, Oregon*

*Dear Mr. Bressler—*

*…Many of the people here who were sent out by the IRO came to me having heard of my arrival, and knowing that I was one of the investigators of the IRO, wish me to thank the IRO for helping them to success in their various occupations by transporting them to Portland. The following are a few names. Mr. Aaron Zaik a recent arrival has a large 2nd hand furniture store. Mr. Lvov or Lvovsky a tinsmith sent out direct 2 years ago has* [illegible] *and a hardware store. Mr. Kaplan, a tailor is earning $20–$25 weekly. Mr. Nathan Siegel who arrived only a few days ago is already employed as a clerk earning $10 for a start, and many others too numerous to mention have succeeded well in a short time.*

*I remain yours respectfully,*

*Alex Grubman*

This letter from Russian immigrant Alex Grubman to the manager of the Industrial Removal Office in New York tells the story of one organization during the great migration wave of the early 1900s. Founded by trustees of the Baron de Hirsch Fund, and working in collaboration with Jewish communities around the country, the IRO dispersed unemployed Jewish immigrants from the Lower East Side of New York to locations with better employment opportunities. Between 1901 and 1922, the IRO sent seventy-nine thousand New Yorkers to 1,700 locations. Several hundred came to Oregon.

The IRO was established in response to the growing concerns of America's established German Jewish population. In 1881, 80,000 Jews lived in New York. By 1901, the number had reached 510,000. New York

Barbur Boulevard replaced the interurban railroad. *Courtesy Colonel Joseph Colasuonno.*

Jewish charitable organizations were going bankrupt, and anti-immigrant legislation threatened. Some worried about an anti-Semitic backlash and even a radical socialist breeding ground in lower New York. The IRO hired lawyer David Bressler as general manager and sent agents around the country to elicit help from local B'nai B'riths.

IRO applicants fell into three categories. "Direct Removals" just wanted to leave New York and accepted any destination. "Request Removals" asked to locate near relatives or friends. "Reunion Removals" joined family and friends previously sent out by the IRO. Frequently the husband came first, and his wife and children followed once he was established.

As elsewhere, Portland's IRO agents found work and housing for the newcomers. Led by Ben Selling, the Hebrew Benevolent Association worked with New York manager David Bressler. When Portland sent the IRO notices of job openings, the IRO responded with information about potential migrants. Letters from applicants and agents archived at the American Jewish Historical Society explain the process and provide a glimpse into this often forgotten organization.

The next three letters show Selling's emphasis on uniting families. They also reveal conditions among the immigrant population. In a 2009 interview, South Portlander Nina Weinstein remarked that a relative told her father that Portland's streets were paved with gold. "When my father came out," she said, "he discovered, definitely, the streets were not paved with gold."

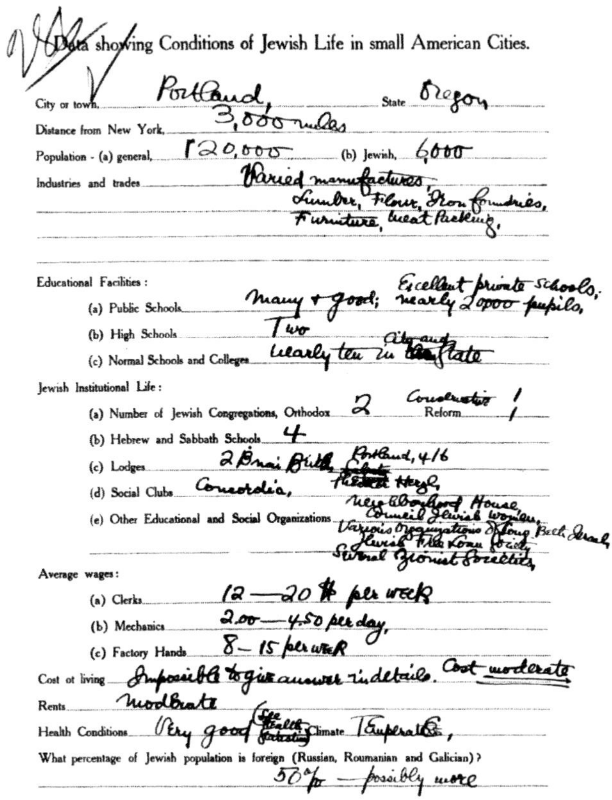

Data showing Conditions of Jewish Life in small American Cities.

City or town Portland, State Oregon

Distance from New York, 3,000 miles

Population - (a) general, 120,000 (b) Jewish, 6000

Industries and trades Varied manufactures, Lumber, Flour, Iron foundries, Furniture, Meat Packing,

Educational Facilities:

(a) Public Schools many + good; Excellent private schools, nearly 20000 pupils,

(b) High Schools Two

(c) Normal Schools and Colleges nearly ten in city and state

Jewish Institutional Life:

(a) Number of Jewish Congregations, Orthodox 2 Conservative 1 Reform 1

(b) Hebrew and Sabbath Schools 4

(c) Lodges 2 Bnai Brith, Portland, 416

(d) Social Clubs Concordia, Herzl,

(e) Other Educational and Social Organizations Neighborhood House, Council Jewish Women, Various Organizations of Cong. Beth Israel, Jewish Free Loan Society, Several Zionist Societies

Average wages:

(a) Clerks 12—20 $ per week

(b) Mechanics 2.00—4.50 per day,

(c) Factory Hands 8–15 per week

Cost of living Impossible to give answer in details. Cost moderate

Rents moderate

Health Conditions Very good Climate Temperate,

What percentage of Jewish population is foreign (Russian, Roumanian and Galician)? 50% — possibly more

The Industrial Removal Office conducted nationwide population surveys. *Courtesy American Jewish Historical Society Industrial Removal Records.*

*July 15, 1908*
*Mr. David M Bressler Mgr*

*Dear Sir*

*Mrs. Freda Weiss, a widow with two children claiming to be a midwife, says she has a daughter aged between 16 & 17 in N York City, who is without friends or money or work—and is exceedingly anxious to have the child, Annie, sent to her claiming that where there is enough for three to eat, there is enough for four. She occupies one room, $4 a month and says she is unable to contribute anything towards transportation. I insisted upon her landlady taking of a collection and today she brings me ten dollars. The mother, who by the way is a clean looking person, is fearful that the* *young girl without money or work might be led astray, and begs to have her sent out here.*

*Owing to lack of time, I am unable to confirm her statements, but the woman has made a good impression on me. The girl could easily obtain employment here. Can you send her? Her address is: Annie Weiss c/o Meyer Meierwitz, 162 Allen Street. That is as near as I can translate the language.*

*Respectfully Yours,*

*Ben Selling*

---

*July 22nd, 1908*
*Mr. Ben Selling,*
*Portland, Oregon*

*Dear Sir:—*

*In response to your letter of the 15th inst. Regarding the application of Mrs. Freda Weiss to have her daughter Annie sent to her, we beg to say that if upon investigation we find no reason for refusing transportation, we will consider the application favorably, if a fair contribution is forthcoming. Can Mrs. Weiss not bring you more than the $10.00 she has already given?*

*Yours very truly,*

*General Manager*

---

*Aug. 5, 1908*
*In re Annie Weiss*

*Her mother called at my request today and says it is utterly impossible for her to raise any more than the ten dollars already on deposit with us. Inasmuch as the child has no male relatives, and is absolutely without any protector, I believe it would be wise to assist her with transportation and send her soon as possible.*

*Respectfully Yours*

*Ben Selling*

In the following letter dated December 2, 1907, Ben Selling refers to *Jewish* tramps (emphasis his). Information about this issue is sketchy. The September 19, 1922 *Oregonian* reported that the Jewish Relief Society, founded in 1908 under David Nemerovsky, and the South Portland Benevolent Society, under Noah Director "concerned themselves with the relief and care of destitute and homeless men, a large number of the cases being transients":

*Portland, Oregon, Dec 2 1907*
*Mr. David M Bressler*

*Dear Sir*

*Enclosed I take pleasure in handing you NY Exchange for two hundred fifty dollars for the transportation of the Cantor family—who arrived here recently. This closes that matter. In re* [illegible name], *I do not advise sending him here at present, nor anyone else whose relatives refuse to pay a reasonable amount toward transportation. Conditions are not favorable here now. One poor fellow committed suicide by drowning last week on account of lack of work. We have been overrun recently with* *<u>Jewish</u>* *Tramps, and it is almost impossible to obtain employment of any kind.*

*Respectfully Yours,*

*Ben Selling*

Everyone remembers South Portland's ubiquitous junk peddlers. Newcomers often borrowed money for a horse and wagon and went into business for themselves. They picked up scrap, bottles, whatever they could find, and sold them to the junk dealers who lined Front Avenue. They eventually organized into the Oregon Junk Peddlers Association and held regular meetings at the Neighborhood House on Southwest Second Avenue:

> *May 12, 1908*
> *Mr. David M. Bressler Mgr*
>
> *Dear Sir*
>
> *Re Joe Feldman, I have again sent for his friend* [illegible name] *who again states his inability to donate anything towards transportation, but is willing to assist him upon his arrival here. So that you may know, I will state that while conditions here are not good, they are not bad. Good tailors or good mechanics can find work of some sort, and times are going to improve.*
>
> *Perhaps you will be interested to know, that the man Kessler with ten children, who you sent out here, after being assisted several times, was loaned money to buy a horse and wagon, and went into the junk peddling business, and is doing well. I loaned him one hundred dollars, payable two dollars a month. He has made two payments and is making an excellent living and some besides.*
>
> *Respectfully Yours*
>
> *Ben Selling*

In many ways an employment agency, the IRO always looked for local opportunities. While Ben Selling and the Hebrew Benevolent Association often filtered these requests, the next two letters show direct correspondence between businesses in Portland and the IRO in New York. In the first, the Zion Meat Market is looking for someone who can slaughter animals according to Jewish religious ritual:

> *August 7th, 1908*
> *Mr. Resnick,*
> *c/o Zion Meat Market*
> *608 First Street,*
> *Portland, Oregon.*

*Dear Sir:—*

*In reply to your letter of July 3rd in conjunction with a letter from Mr. Adler, we beg to say that we have not at present a shochet upon our list, and regret therefore to be unable to send a suitable man to you. However, if you will communicate with Rabbi L. Drachman, 36 East 75th Street, New York City, he may know of a shochet who would be able to accept the position you have.*

*Very truly yours,*

*General Manager.*

*Oct. 20th 1909*
*Hebrew Charity Association*
*New York N.Y.*

*Gentlemen:—*

*We are conducting a factory here, making Cigarettes by hand. We are in need of the services of one or two good, all around Cigarette Makers. They must understand their business thoroughly and must know how to make mouthpiece as well as cork tip cigarettes. To such we are able to offer steady work at good pay, which of course is piecework. For their information, we beg to say that we have a large Jewish population in this city supporting four Synagogues.*

*Thanking you in advance for your kindness in the matter we beg to remain, Gentlemen,*

*Yours Very Truly,*
*F Geller Cigarette Factory*
*By A.R. Roberts, Secy.*

The IRO expected most applicants to pay at least part of the transportation costs. It often lent additional money and was paid back with mixed results:

*May 8th, 1908*
*Mr. Ben Selling*
*Portland, Ore.*

*Dear Mr. Selling:—*

*I have yours of the 30th ult requesting us to grant transportation to Joseph and Anna* [illegible]. *They have long been applicants here for transportation but our investigation in the case does not incline us favorably to their request. Their application was full of incorrect statements, particularly with respect to their connections, and I feel that we are not doing them any injustice in declining to send them. Still, in view of your recommendation, we are willing to do considerable for them, but we will not send them gratis. They will have to contribute at least $50 toward the expense of their transportation.*

*With kind regards, I am,*

*Yours very truly,*

*General Manager*

---

*Feb. 5th, 1907*
*Mr. Ben Selling,*
*Portland, Ore.*

*My Dear Mr. Selling:—*

*I have your favor of the 19th, ult. and in answer there to beg to say that it has never been the policy of this Society to aid any one not a bona fide resident of New York City. People going to some city in the interior of the United States and paying their transportation only as far as New York are not considered proper applicants. Our movement has for one of its purposes the diversion of immigration from New York, and to promote such, and we have sent from New York City thousands of people to the interior where there were better opportunities for them to earn a livelihood, so that their relatives and friends might join them in their new homes instead of coming to New York, as would have been the case otherwise. It could hardly be construed as serving this purpose for us to send people whose destination is Cincinnati or Portland, Ore., and who simply stop off in New York for any reason whatsoever. We must discourage any attempt on the part of people whose destination is elsewhere to stop in New York. They should go straight on to their destination, and if they haven't enough money to pay their transportation, they should be discouraged from starting from their native home until they or those whom they are going to join have accumulated enough money to pay for the entire transportation. It is a matter of absolute fact that there have been many people living in the interior of the United States, who, knowing of the existence of the Removal Office, have sent just enough money to enable their relatives to come as far as New York, relying upon the Removal Office to send them further, notwithstanding the fact that they had or could have obtained enough money to pay for their entire transportation themselves.*

*I know that in the case of Portland we have made an exception or two, and really for no very good reason, excepting your intercession. If at any time, an immigrant whose destination is some point in the interior finds himself stranded in New York City, due to unavoidable circumstances, we will come to his assistance, but otherwise we must confine our activities to bona fide residents of New York City.*

*Yours very sincerely,*

*General Manager*

## A 1940s Social Worker's World

Indelible memories of the 1940s remain with everyone who lived through those turbulent times. As Hitler's refugees poured into the United States, Jewish federations across the country mobilized to help. The stories of one survivor and a federation social worker provide insight into Portland's own postwar community.

Lillian Kessler Wexler (1924–2007) became the Federated Jewish Societies of Portland caseworker after graduating from Reed College in

Lillian Kessler Wexler (left) and Vivienne Goldberg Bonnin celebrate Victory in Japan Day on August 14, 1945. *Courtesy Vivienne Goldberg Bonnin.*

1945. Born in the Bronx, New York, to Viennese immigrants, she and her family moved to Oregon in 1943 and landed in the South Portland immigrant neighborhood. She recalled her experience in an oral history taken a few years before her death.

"I never got over the feeling that there but for the grace of God go I," she said about her work with Portland's refugee community. "My parents got out of Europe in the nick of time. Any family they had, were gone."

At that time, all of the federation agencies had offices at the Jewish Community Center on Southwest Thirteenth Avenue. Social services organizations had not coalesced. "They had one administrator, Mrs. Julia Swett, and one caseworker—me," Wexler said. "The agency was divided into pieces, and each did its own thing. Even my paycheck came in pieces. Temple [Beth Israel] people served on the boards. They did all the high-level stuff."

Wexler said that national Jewish organizations like the Hebrew Immigrant Aid Society and Joint Distribution Committee dispersed European refugees throughout the country. She called her work with the immigrants "phenomenally intense."

While decades later, the settlement of Soviet refugees drew scores of volunteers, Wexler remembered working alone. She picked up people at the train depot, found housing and medical care. She brought welfare checks to federation president Max Hirsch for signatures each Friday. "I reported why people were still on assistance," she said. "We offered jobs to most refugees when they came. Some chose to take them, and some didn't."

Since most refugees didn't speak English, Wexler's knowledge of Yiddish proved vital. "The tough ones were families who came from Italy," she said. She teared up when she remembered one. "The only apartment I could find the family was on the east side on a busy street," she said. "When the man complained of headaches, everyone said it was psychosomatic—he's not used to the noise. Eventually, a volunteer doctor referred him to a neurologist. It was a brain tumor. His widow said, 'He lived through the war, and through the concentration camps. He finally got to where he could be free.' I think it was six weeks from arrival to burial."

Ruth Lindemann, the daughter of Austrian survivors, remembers her father speaking of Wexler with reverence. "He'd say, 'I have to go see Mrs. Wexler.' I could tell by his voice that he thought she was very helpful," she said. Lindemann married another survivor whom she met at the Friendship Club. Held at the federation-sponsored Neighborhood House, this organization became central for Holocaust survivors.

"The Friendship Club was a real catalyst," she said. "Everyone in our circle met their spouses there. We usually had food and dancing—tangos, foxtrots. They had a dance contest, which Fred and I usually won. Most people spoke German. Some went to services and some were not that observant, so it was a good place to get together."

Like many who found themselves trapped in Europe, her husband's family fled to Shanghai, China, where Jews could go without visas. They stayed for nine years. "In Shanghai, his father learned to make umbrellas," Lindemann said. "And the Jewish committee that was helping place people thought Portland was a good place for an umbrella maker."

The Lindemann family came to Portland in 1948. "The Jewish Community Center had a refugee settlement and a job-finding organization," she said. "They found an apartment for them on Northwest Northrup Street. Several refugee families were there. We knew at least twenty families who had been in Shanghai. We met at the Friendship Club."

# SOVIET JEWS MOVE TO PORTLAND

Khasya Grossman left Ukraine in 1978 and wrote home about green, clean Portland. When her granddaughter, Raisa Premysler, and her family arrived two years later, they expected a beautiful scene. Instead, dirt covered everything along the way to the downtown apartment that Jewish Family and Child Service had arranged.

"We walked to the Rose Festival Parade and had trouble breathing," Premysler said. People wore facemasks. Strangers smiled. "Grandma's brain is gone," she told her husband, referring to her grandmother's letter. "Half the people here have tuberculosis, and the other half are crazy."

Of course, the Premyslers laughed when they learned about Mount St. Helen's recent eruption. Still, adjusting to their new country took longer. From learning English to understanding a capitalist society, Soviet immigrants faced significant challenges.

Raisa and Isaac Premysler came to America from the Soviet Union in 1980. *Photo by author.*

According to Jewish Family and Child Service, about two thousand Jews from the Former Soviet Union settled in Portland between the 1970s and 1990s. The Soviet invasion of Afghanistan and President Jimmy Carter's subsequent boycott of the 1980 Moscow Olympics halted the initial wave. Emigration resumed after the breakup of the Soviet Union.

Premysler came with the first wave. "I had my share of anti-Semitism," she said. "I didn't want this to happen to our daughter. We knew life was better in America, but that wasn't the main thing. By Russian standards, we lived OK. We had a nice apartment with indoor plumbing."

Premysler remembered growing up Jewish in Ukraine. Her grandfather prayed behind closed blinds. Communist party membership was a prerequisite for educational and employment opportunities but was barred to the religiously observant. Degrees of anti-Semitism varied by location. When her parents warned that Ukrainian universities would not admit a Jew, she studied medicine near the Ural Mountains.

JFCS Russian resettlement coordinator Carol Chestler met the Premyslers at the airport in 1980. Portland's first FSU immigrants arrived during her presidency at the Portland Section of the National Council of Jewish Women. "The federation [Jewish Federation of Greater Portland] asked us to be the volunteer arm of the program," she said. "The Hebrew Immigrant Aid Society channeled Russian Jews around the country…Our goal was to get them self-sufficient as soon as possible. HIAS got funds from the federal government and apportioned amounts through the JFGP. That's how we paid for the first three months."

The JFCS registered children for school and enrolled families in programs like food stamps. Chestler helped set up a medical clinic at St. Vincent's hospital and arranged for English and citizenship classes. Portlanders stepped in to help. Without English language skills and United States qualifications, many immigrants could not initially work in their professions. Local businesses found jobs to tide them over. In a project that grew into today's Community Warehouse, JFCS collected used furniture and supplies. Throughout those hectic times, the volunteer-in-charge, Bernice Rosencranz, answered the phone with "How many are coming?" instead of "Hello."

Other volunteers helped newcomers overcome culture shock. For example, on a visit to Albertsons, an FSU family commented on how low-income the neighborhood must be. "Why?" the volunteer asked. "Because," they said, "all the shelves are full."

Chestler also remembers a misconception. "The community assumed that the only reason [FSU immigrants] came was to practice their religion. That was important to some but not everyone. They wanted a job; they wanted their kids to have a good education; they wanted a comfortable life. And they wanted to say they were Jews without anyone discriminating against them. They were so courageous to leave their country and start a new life."

Rita and Mark Shmulevsky, who immigrated in 1988, agree. "We had an internal passport—it's like a driver's license," Rita Shmulevsky said, remembering life in the FSU. "It had your name, date of birth and nationality—Jewish. Everywhere we went, we had to show the passport. To buy tickets for a train, you showed it. All this anti-Semitism…to get into college, you needed to be the best. If you want a promotion at work—as a Jew, you didn't have a chance."

Although Jewish identity remained strong, interest in religion waned under the Soviet regime. "My mom's family were rabbis for generations," Mark Shmulevsky said. "For Passover, our grandmother would go to the synagogue, wait in line and get a little matzo. We didn't read the Haggadah, but we had dinner."

When four generations of the Shmulevsky family arrived in Portland, the *Jewish Review* ran a full-page story. The two-bedroom apartment the JFCS rented for them seemed opulent. Now they needed jobs and fast. "We didn't have interviews in Russia," Rita Shmulevsky said. "We had a single employer—the government. My friend created one hundred questions in English with answers regarding my job experience. I memorized it."

A computer programmer trained in a popular English language database, Shmulevsky soon saw an opportunity with the city. Although she couldn't understand complete sentences, she spouted memorized answers at the sound of any familiar word. They hired her. Mark Shmulevsky, who had an advanced degree in computer science, also continued in his profession.

Like the Shmulevskys, Vera Goldman arrived during the second wave of Soviet emigration. "There were education quotas, job quotas; Jews never got high government positions," she said.

Born in the early 1900s, Goldman's parents came from traditional backgrounds. They lived in shtetls, spoke Yiddish and not Russian and followed religious tradition. "During the Sabbath, Russian ladies took the food off their stove and prepared it," Goldman said. "My father told stories about the cheder."

Tradition all but disappeared under the Soviets. "Few people knew my mother listened to the Yiddish radio because it was dangerous." Goldman said. "We didn't have a synagogue, but a minyon had permission to meet at someone's house. During Passover, some Russian people made the matzo. My father was a member of the communist party, so he couldn't go buy it. My mother went."

Goldman became a junior college math instructor. She emigrated in 1990 at age fifty-five and vowed to remain independent. Hired as an educational assistant for Portland Public Schools, she later trained and taught English as a Second Language. "I was in *Who's Who American Teachers* in 1998," she said. "For the past twenty years, I've been an American."

*Part II*

# THE NEIGHBORHOOD GANG

Some compare First Street in South Portland with Delancy Street on New York's Lower East Side. The self-contained community had everything Jewish immigrants might need. There were kosher butchers, bagel makers, a fish market and even a barbershop where "Dr. Wolfe" applied leeches. The Neighborhood House gave citizenship and English classes. After work, men sat on apple boxes outside the grocery and discussed "Bintel Brief," an advice column in the Yiddish press.

Most people say that the neighborhood was one-third Jewish, one-third Italian and one-third everything else, including a small African American population and, at one time, Roma, or Gypsies. The Jewish population came from Eastern Europe often by way of New York—or from Turkey and Greece by way of Seattle. Synagogues flourished. Their nicknames reflected their location or their congregants' country of origin. The Kazatzker Shul membership came from Russia. Many who grew up attending the First Street Shul didn't know that the "real" name was Shaarie Torah.

Although most South Portlanders did not feel deprived, the perception outside the neighborhood told a different story. A July 15, 1914 *Morning Oregonian* article under the headline "Slum Conditions Probed" described Mayor Albee and the city commissioners' investigation into substandard housing. "They were taken to South Portland and to the Albina district, where many complaints of poor condition [*sic*] have been made," the article noted. "Bad conditions were found in several places. Large families in small,

Josef and Adele Etlinger in 1930. *Courtesy Norman and Judy Rosenbloom.*

Early Failing School graduation class. Principal Fanny Porter (third row, left) was dedicated to Americanizing the children. *Courtesy Anita Gold.*

ill-smelling rooms without outside light or ventilation and with poor sanitary conditions were discovered."

A September 24, 1916 article headlined "Park Plan Favored, Citizens in Other Parts Give Way to South Portland, Garbage Heaps and Streets Only Places Youngsters Have Now for Playgrounds" went on to say that "residents of other sections are concurring in Commissioner Baker's plan to cut out many needed improvements elsewhere and put the money into the South Portland project." The effort resulted in Duniway Park.

By the 1920s, Jews started leaving South Portland for more prestigious east side neighborhoods like Laurelhurst and Irvington. A series of highway projects—including the Ross Island Bridge in 1926, Barbur Boulevard construction and Front Avenue expansion in the 1930s, as well as freeway

South Portlander Hal Boren in front of Tom Stern's garage on Southwest Fourth. *Courtesy Bonnie Boren.*

Many thought that First Avenue in South Portland was like Delancy Street on the Lower East Side of New York, 1954. *Courtesy City of Portland Archives, Oregon, Korsun's Kosher Delicatessen. A2005-005.*

construction in the early 1960s—leveled parts of the neighborhood and divided others. The 1958 South Auditorium Urban Renewal project demolished fifty-four blocks in favor of new high-rises. By that time, South Portland had relatively fewer Jewish children and more Jewish seniors than other parts of the city, according to historian Dr. William Toll.

Still, many never forgot the closeness and excitement of their early immigrant neighborhood. Mention Hebrew school, the Neighborhood House, basketball or the ubiquitous junk peddlers and photographs come out and stories are retold. Lifelong friendships grew from the small town atmosphere. There will never be another South Portland.

# GRANDPA WAS A WASTEPAPER PICKER

My grandfather was a wastepaper picker. He emigrated from Vilna in the early 1900s, settled in Waterbury, Connecticut and eventually set up a box factory in his backyard. Maybe that's why I'm crazy about junk peddler stories and why South Portland is a place after my own heart, as my British husband would say.

In 1910, virtually every junk peddler in Portland was Jewish and lived in the immigrant neighborhood. Many people I've talked to remember when they called recyclers "junk peddlers" and when horses and wagons plied the streets of South Portland. The late Gussie Reinhardt often spoke of the "original recyclers" who kept their horses in her parents' barn on Southwest Meade Street.

"The men who brought the horses and wagons into the barn would go to the top area, leave the wagons and walk the horses down to their stalls in the lower level," she said. "The peddlers paid three dollars a month. There were about twenty horses, and it was a big help."

There were other barns. Former police detective Norman Rosenbloom's grandfather kept horses in the dirt basement of his home around the corner from Reinhardt's. Portland accountant Leo Greenstein remembered Fox's barn, where his father kept Bill, the horse who pulled his wagon.

"My father was a junk peddler," Greenstein said in a 2004 interview. "He woke up at 7:00 and had cereal—mush for breakfast. He'd go harness up the horse and pick up things at people's houses or businesses—bottles, things like that. Once in a while, he'd pick up an antique and make a little extra."

Greenstein also remembered the Oregon Junk Peddlers Association that met at the Neighborhood House. An October 10, 1928 *Oregonian* article under the headline "Junkmen Get Charter, Gevurtz Hall Jammed with Jubilant Celebrants" reported the group's founding ceremony at South Portland's Jewish meeting hall:

> *Standing room was at a premium and more than 200 persons were turned away Wednesday night, when members of the recently organized Oregon Junk Peddlers' Association held open house in Gevurtz Hall on Front and Gibbs streets. Mayor George L. Baker attended along with representatives from the police. The association's president, Mr. H. Harris, addressed the crowd in Yiddish and English.*

"It was the Depression, and peddlers like my dad were having a hard time," Greenstein said. "The main objective was to get a reduction in the license fee. One leader was a grocer on Southwest Front. And the mother of the man who was mayor at one time lived in our neighborhood. She got him to help."

Like other junk peddlers, Greenstein's father sold what he collected to the junk dealers who lined Front Avenue. "When people needed a new tool or something for the house, they'd shop secondhand first," Greenstein said. "And the dealers sold scrap to metal refineries."

Flora Rigotti remembered growing up in the Italian bachelor's boardinghouse next to Alaska Junk, owned by Sam Schnitzer and Harry Wolfe. "It was a busy place, with horses and wagons piled with scrap iron and a large wooden barnlike building," she said. "They kept bolts of damaged goods in the loft upstairs. That's how our mother made our school dresses.

Josef and Adele Etlinger immigrated to Portland from Eastern Europe. Their granddaughter, Judy Rosenbloom, keeps baby Louie's white dress framed on her wall. *Courtesy Norman and Judy Rosenbloom.*

She picked out something fairly decent. We each got one dress for winter and one for summer."

Judy Rosenbloom's family lived in the house still standing at 013 Southwest Arthur Street. Her grandfather, Joseph Etlinger, left Austria when threatened with conscription. "The family came to Portland, and he was a junk dealer," she said. Later, her father and uncle opened the Ace Trading secondhand store on Southwest First Avenue. "It was totally disorganized. You couldn't say the tools were in this section or the furniture in that. But if somebody came in and asked for something, they went right to it."

Rosenbloom's and Greenstein's families left the junk business long ago, but those who remained could find lasting returns. Todd Rosenthal is fourth-generation owner of American Rag and Metal. His great-grandfather left Lodz, Poland, stopped in Philadelphia and brought the business across the country with him. He arrived in Portland about 1940 and started with Rosenthal's Trading Post on Southwest Second Avenue.

Ken Unkeles remembered the American Rag and Metal factory in Northwest Portland, just one block from his family's carton business. He still keeps his real estate office in the 1904 warehouse.

"Our big account was Blitz Brewery," Unkeles said. "Every morning we'd go there at 6:00 a.m. and pick up pallets of boxes. Twice a week, when they ran returnable quarts, we got in front of the garbage. We got the boxes, took them back to our warehouse and resold them. We processed ten thousand boxes a week."

"Every Unkeles from my age up was in the junk business," he continued. "Grandfather started with a horse and wagon. When Zeyde died, my uncle asked me to run the route. We started up the truck, went to as many places as we could remember and picked up junk. I put myself through college doing this. That pickup truck was a great inheritance."

## ESTHER CHERNICHOWSKY: A MEMOIR

*The Neighborhood House Hebrew School comes up fast during any discussion of Old South Portland. Children attended one of three sessions after school Monday through Thursday and on Sunday mornings. On Friday evenings and Saturday mornings, the students led services at the Jewish Old People's Home. All went under the watchful eye of school*

H.I. Chernichowsky served as the Portland Hebrew School principal from 1931 to the early 1950s. *Courtesy Marcia Ketzlach Gale.*

*principal Mr. Hayim Isaac Chernichowsky (circa 1890–1955). The former principal of the Seattle Talmud Torah, he took up his post in 1931 and remained until the early 1950s. His daughter, Esther Chernichowsky Ketzlach, grew up in South Portland and attended Shattuck School, Lincoln High, Reed College and UCLA. This 2009 interview was by phone from her home in Los Angeles.*

It was a one-man operation. My father recruited the teachers, supervised the curriculum and oversaw the finances. He got financing from Jews who didn't have much to do with the Hebrew school, but they had the money.

My father was from a small town near Minsk in western Russia. Right after his Bar Mitzvah, his mother died and his father remarried. They sent him to a Yeshiva, and he didn't have a home to speak of after that.

Later, he didn't want to serve in the army, so when the revolution broke out, he went to Siberia. They'd either capture you for the communists or for the czar.

He met my mother in Kabansk, Siberia. They married in December 1919. My mother's family had been in Siberia for generations. Her grandfather had been captured by the czar's army and served for twenty-five years. As a result, they permitted him to own land, and he chose Siberia. Everyone assumes Siberia is the place they send prisoners, but actually it is a rich country. It's like the Wild West. It's got timber, oil, all kinds of reserves and, especially, the fur industry.

My great-grandparents were pioneers, but their children became wealthy and did well until the communists came. They dealt in furs, owned a cannery and exported leather all over the world. My mother was one of thirteen

H.I., Braina and Esther Chernichowsky shortly after their 1925 arrival in the United States. *Courtesy Marcia Ketzlach Gale.*

children. She became an assistant doctor, or felcher, for the army medical corps. I guess it was for the czar because they surely weren't communists. When the communists came in and fought the White Russians, Jews were caught in the middle. My father was an outspoken anticommunist and a religious man, so he was between the devil and the deep blue sea.

I was a couple days old when we escaped to Manchuria, China. We lived in a kehila-type community made up mostly of Russian Jews. They had their own government and their own rules. In 1925, when I was four, we came to Seattle and stayed until I was ten. Then my father got a job as the Portland Hebrew School principal. It was a one-man operation—he would have more autonomy, and he liked that.

We lived on Southwest Tenth Avenue between College and Jackson. It was a nice community. We went to the Sixth Street Shul, Neveh Tzedek, for twenty-five years. We often had an early dinner and walked over to one of the movie houses. In the summer, we'd take our dinners to Mount Tabor Park with friends.

We went to the beach at Rockaway during July and August. There were little houses, and our friends occupied them. On Saturday evenings a band came. If there wasn't anyone to dance with, we'd dance with each other.

Portland had a good Hebrew school, one of the best in the country, I understand. We went five days a week. My father had a lot of patience with the kids, but he did have a temper. He was a disciplinarian. He hated kids who were smart alecky. He couldn't abide kids who were spoiled and arrogant. They learned early on not to push him too far.

The school was his life. He grew up in Russia and always had dreams of becoming a farmer in Israel. In his free time, he liked to putter in the backyard and plant tomatoes and other things. And he always did the shopping. Where he grew up, they didn't have a lot of food, so he liked to buy the best. He bought vegetables and fruits in the stalls at the Fifth Street Market. We got chickens from the kosher butcher, Mr. Schnitzer.

When I asked my father about Russia, he would say, "Deep mud and a lot of trouble." But my mother talked about the old country a lot. In Siberia, she lived in a big house with plenty of help. Here she was a good housekeeper, but she didn't take great pride in it. That was not her bag.

Russian was her main language, but she read English well. After she married my father, she learned Jewish, and we had a huge Yiddish library—all the classics. She loved to work with needles. She crocheted and embroidered. In Siberia, there wasn't a lot for them to do, so they learned intricate handwork. I still have afghans she made.

## Harold Saltzman: A Memoir

*Harold Saltzman (1925–2011) served as the Jewish Federation of Greater Portland's president during the Six-Day War. He grew up in South Portland, attended the University of Oregon and became a Hall of Fame pitcher before retiring to his lumber business. The "Tom Stern" he mentions in his interview was the father of Jerry Stern, a well-known Portland philanthropist and fellow South Portlander.*

We lived on Third Street between College and Lincoln, near the Jewish Old People's Home. My parents rented the house for twenty dollars a month. One of the great things was, it had a fireplace that burned sawdust. That was a step up from wood. During the winter, my brother and I argued about who would fill it.

My parents emigrated from Russia. My mother came here because the Cossacks attacked their village a couple times. My grandmother grabbed my mother and aunt and hid out in the woods.

My father came from a large family, and it was tough living. He ran away twice to come to the States, but his father got him back somehow. Then my father told him, "If you don't let me go to the States, I'm gonna become a goy." And, my grandfather said, "Heaven forbid. Here, take this money and go."

He landed on Ellis Island and worked his way across country. He knew little English, so when he went to get jobs he said yes to everything. He worked on a farm, on a fishing boat and in the copper mines of Alaska—all from saying yes.

While he was in Alaska, he saw Portland, Oregon, on a map. He'd made enough money to come by train. When he got here, a man who hauled luggage took him home for dinner. He lived with them for three years. That was the Tom Stern family.

My father was, well, they call them recyclers now, but he was a junkman. He didn't talk about his business because he didn't want my brother and me

*Right*: South Portlander Hal Saltzman pitched for the Beavers at Vaughn Street Park in 1949. *Courtesy Portland Interscholastic League Hall of Fame.*

*Below*: Hal Saltzman outside his South Portland home, circa 1927. *Courtesy Ruth Saltzman.*

to go into it. He had a Dodge truck and picked up scrap from five companies and sold it. He was with them for more than thirty years. Every Christmas my mother put on a lunch with corned beef, and the people he dealt with came over. One time I asked Mr. Wills, who was the president of Cummins Diesel, "How do you trust my dad so much." He said, "Because he's an honest man."

My father played pinochle in the afternoon. He was not particularly ambitious. He didn't want to be a tycoon, but he made a decent living. He and my mother belonged to ICOR [Association for Jewish Colonization in the Soviet Union], an organization that helped Jews get to Birobidzhan. That was the wonderful territory in Siberia that Stalin gave them. ICOR had a picnic once a year at Sellwood Park. A lot of people turned out, but most were poor and couldn't do much. This was in the late '30s.

South Portland was mainly Jews and Italians. The Italians were great. When we lived on Caruthers, our neighbors sold bootleg wine until prohibition was removed. We only knew two black people. One was called Flash and the other was Smokey. Both were good athletes. On First and Sheridan, right near Calistro and Halperin, there was an apartment where only black people lived. It was a firetrap.

A lot of the students at Shattuck School were Oriental. They lived east of school, within six or ten blocks. Their parents were either in the restaurant business or cleaning. I really don't remember. After classes, the Oriental kids went to Chinese or Japanese school, and the Jewish kids went to Hebrew school.

Hebrew school was at the Neighborhood House on Second Avenue. I went for just three days. They had these Russian instructors that carried little sticks around. If you played around, they whacked you. I got whacked a couple times because my cousin and I were talking or something, so instead of going to Hebrew school we'd just go to the gym and play ball.

What did we do after school? I remember going down to the First Street Shul. We rolled nuts as close as we could to the curb. Whoever got the closest collected the nuts. And we played softball at Lair Hill Park. The league was made up according to the size. Four feet, ten inches was the ceiling. There was a tennis court, but few people played. It was a rich man's game, almost like golf.

I fell in love with frozen Snickers bars at Berg's theater on First and Grant. For ten or fifteen cents, you got a double bill, a serial and either a *March of Time* or a cartoon. A serial is like a TV show that continues. The B'nai B'rith

Jewish National Fund Golden Book Certificate, December 3, 1967. *From left*: Rabbi Joshua Stampfer, Harold Saltzman, Ruth Saltzman, Shirley Tanzer, Hershal Tanzer, Rabbi Emanuel Rose, A.E. Rosenberg and an unidentified Israeli official. *Courtesy Ruth Saltzman.*

center had a club called the Cardinals, and we played basketball with the Neighborhood House team. All the boys belonged to AZA [Aleph Zadik Aleph]. We had basketball games with Seattle.

The first athletic team I played for was St. Lawrence. It was a Catholic church on Third and Sheridan. I can't remember the priest's name, but he was a terrific guy who coached this little kids' football team. We played at Duniway Park. It was a bowl, and the northeast corner was home plate. They had lights for softball games, and they drew big crowds. Later, they filled in the bowl and made a running track.

Running was not like it is today. It was baseball and softball then. In the winter, there'd be touch tackle football. Young guys played—no uniforms. You just put on your old clothes.

# NINA WEINSTEIN: A MEMOIR

*Nina Weinstein (born 1915) grew up in South Portland's heyday, with Yiddish spoken on the streets and villagers from the old country around the corner. During this 2009 interview, she referred to well-known people and institutions. "The original Mr. Schnitzer," who owned her family's first home, was Sam Schnitzer. He came to Portland as a junk peddler, graduated to a downtown scrap metal dealership and became one of the city's leading entrepreneurs. Mrs. Benjamin Selling (Matilda) was the wife of Ben Selling (1852–1931), a respected businessman and philanthropist. Among his accomplishments, he served as state senator and president of the Hebrew Benevolent Association, founded a university scholarship fund and opened soup kitchens during the Depression. Tillie Selling belonged to the National Council of Jewish Women. She presided over the Neighborhood House Sewing School for thirty-two years. Nina Weinstein attended Commerce High, became a credit manager and married a man who also had the name Weinstein. They had three children. She lives in Eugene, Oregon.*

My parents came from Ukraine, near Kiev. My father left for America first in 1903 or 1904. He went to New York but ended up in Cambridge, Massachusetts, where my mother had two sisters. He worked with the longshoremen because they paid the most. It took three years to earn enough money to send for her.

It's a sad story. He left my mother with three children, and when she got off the boat, she only brought two. She felt she could never write and tell him they had lost a child. I don't know which was worse: writing or just presenting the two children.

My uncle from Boston visited Portland and said the streets were paved with gold. When my father came out, he discovered, definitely, the streets were not paved with gold. To me, the amazing thing is, they discovered two families from the same village on their street.

We had no relatives here, but the people from the same village were so close that I often felt they were my relatives. I thought the oldest one was my grandmother. Mrs. Kulchinsky—she lived on one side of the street, and her son and cousin lived across the street. Another family was named Rosen. Mrs. Rosen was a dressmaker. Everybody in town went to her. She was fantastic. In this day and age, she'd be a designer.

Portland had a smaller Jewish community in those days. I could walk in South Portland and tell you the name of everybody who lived in every house.

Nina Weinstein's mother and sisters outside their home on Southwest Hooker Street in South Portland, circa 1914. *Courtesy Nina Weinstein.*

Temple Beth Israel was mostly German Jews who were not only wealthier but thought they were a cut above the Russians. The German Jews came to Portland first. They started small but ended up with big stores like Meier and Frank. Every Jewish girl worked for Meier and Frank growing up. When my oldest sister worked there, she won their beauty contest.

We lived on the right side of the tracks. My mother always let us know. At first, my folks lived in an upstairs flat on Second and Arthur. They rented from the original Mr. Schnitzer. I don't know when they moved to Hooker Street, where I was born. My father couldn't afford to buy the house himself, so the Judkises lived upstairs. There was no kitchen up there, so my mother cooked for both families. I didn't realize this until she told me years later. There was so much about my mother we didn't know. She lent money to women in the neighborhood, and we never knew because she was afraid we might taunt them.

My father had been in the czar's army. He left Russia because the Russo-Japanese war was in the air, and he knew he would be recalled. So he snuck out. Every immigrant tells the same story. At midnight, you bribed the guard.

Later, on hot summer nights, my father sat on the front porch, and kids from the neighborhood came. Remember, we didn't have TV. Kids played in those days. My mother always had something—watermelon or corn on the cob. We sat and listened to my father tell his tales about when he was in the czar's army.

He had a little tailoring shop and sold men's clothing. It was called a workman's shop in those days. The lumberjacks came into town in the winter. There were quite a few Russians. They got a hotel room and got drunk. Many didn't speak English.

My father involved himself in politics. He tried to tell the immigrants that they should become citizens. He was an activist and an interpreter for the courts. He spoke a few Russian and Ukrainian dialects. He also started one of the synagogues here—Linath Hazedek, the Kazatzker Shul. When he finally retired, they gave him a candelabra. It says, "In appreciation for being president of this synagogue." It doesn't say Linath Hazedek because they couldn't spell it. I gave it to my niece.

He was also either president or secretary of the Rose City Lodge. As I understand it, that was a precursor to health insurance. Years later, I spoke to a man who said, "They used to pay us one dollar a day if we were sick."

By the time I belonged, the Rose City Lodge didn't have health benefits. They gave the Yom Kippur dances. When I was growing up, the women wore formals. It was the Depression. Men didn't wear tuxes, they just wore dark blue suits. My friend sent a gardenia, which you wore on your wrist. It was a big thing. If you didn't get invited to the dance, you were a real wallflower.

There were other big Jewish dances during the winter, often in what is now the art museum. It was the Masonic temple in those days. It had a big dance floor and a sunken ballroom. It was a nice thing to have. It's too bad it went by the by.

Jewish weddings were wonderful. There were no babysitters in those days. When you went to a wedding, you took your little kids with you. Before we went, we had to sit down and eat so that we wouldn't become pigs at the wedding. My mother had her own rules. Girls didn't whistle—girls didn't do a lot of things. Girls didn't make pigs of themselves at weddings, so we had to eat at home first. But we did get soda pop.

A lot of the weddings were in Gevurtz Hall. It was upstairs from Zak's grocery on the corner of Gibbs and Front. Mr. Wintler had a drugstore across the street. Somebody organized a birthday party when he was one hundred years old. All the kids from Failing School and a lot of us from Holman came. Most of us were married and had our own children. He was the neighborhood druggist. During the war, I lived on Corbett Street with my mother and baby. I think he cut his thumb. I picked him up and ran to Mr. Wintler's drugstore.

Nina Weinstein and her son outside her mother's home on Southwest Corbett Avenue. *Courtesy Nina Weinstein.*

We moved to Corbett Street between Gaines and Pennoyer when I was three or four. We lived along the streetcar line, and my father's store was on First and Columbia along the tracks. My mother sent my father his lunch every day. She put me on the streetcar when I was like four years old with this basket. My father would be at the other end of the streetcar line and take me and the basket off and then cross the street and put me on the streetcar going back. My mother waited at the other end. The conductors watched out for me.

In those days, the Jewish stores were all on First. There were five or six Jewish groceries, two Jewish bakeries and, I think, five Jewish butcher shops. My mother came down to First Street to do her shopping. There were other groceries stores where I lived, but she insisted on going to Mrs. Maccoby because she was a widow and she was Jewish.

In those days, they shopped two or three times a week and schlepped it on their back all the way home. Before it was developed, Front Street was Produce Row. They had live chickens. My mother would buy a live chicken and take it to the shochet and have him kill it. A poor, little old lady named Shifra would flick it—remove the feathers.

My mother always walked. We said, "Mom, for a nickel you could ride the streetcar." She said, "I wouldn't think of it. What if the chicken squawked?" So she walked with this live chicken, which probably weighed seven or eight pounds.

She didn't cook like most Jewish women. When people say, "What do you attribute your longevity to?" I honestly think it was because my mother unknowingly gave us this wonderful diet. We had very few sweets. Our desserts usually consisted of fruit. We had fruit trees, and she canned everything. In the summer, we had fresh fruit, not just from the trees. Frank the farmer came to our house. My mother was the first one on his route so she got the brown eggs, and he brought all kinds of whatever was in season. She bought a sack of potatoes, a sack of onions and a box of apples. And when that was gone, he supplied her again. Besides Frank the farmer, we had an Italian vegetable man. He came every other day and parked his truck. All the neighbors came to buy vegetables.

On Shabbat, my mother and her cronies met after synagogue. They had a little glass of tea and cookies, and they reminisced and laughed. It was all in Yiddish. I understood everything because my mother spoke only Yiddish to us. They had such wonderful times reminiscing, but I don't recall the stories.

The Neighborhood House was wonderful. I went to sewing school there every Monday after school. Mrs. Selling was the principal. She was tiny woman, and she wore this black ribbon with this gorgeous diamond. Even as a child, I knew it was something.

When you went to sewing school, the first thing you learned was to thread a needle. The next thing you learned was to make a knot with no tail. This took two or three weeks. Once you did that, they gave you a gingham patch to learn your stitches. So, the little square was the running stitch, and the big square was the basting stitch. You did a few stitches and showed them to your teacher. If they were perfect, you made a few more stitches. If they weren't perfect, you had to rip it out. You had a book with your name on it, and when your patch was perfect, you put it in your book.

We took the red train to go to Hillsboro for our summer vacation. There was one Jewish family, and he owned a little store. They had no children, so they were happy to have these three little girls come and spend a week with them. Most of the Jews went to either Seaside or Long Beach, but we always went to Rockaway. My mother not only took a suitcase, she took all her kosher dishes and pots and pans because there was nothing Jewish at the coast. The Jewish butcher in Portland sent us our meat every Thursday by bus.

Nina Weinstein at home in 2011. *Photo by author.*

# THE NEIGHBORHOOD BASKETBALL TEAM

It all started in settlement houses, the community centers of East Coast immigrant districts. According to *The First Basket*, a Jewish basketball documentary, Jewish participation in sports was the greatest change between old world and new. The Neighborhood House in Old South Portland followed that tradition as shown in a 1930s photo of its South Parkway Team.

Two people in the photograph are still alive. Harold Mink holds the basketball. Behind him, right, Ike Donin, is now the University of Oregon's oldest varsity athlete, having lettered in basketball and baseball. Both fondly remember their great coach, Bob Mudrick, pictured top right, who passed away in 1983. Mudrick's brother, Larry, may be Portland's oldest practicing dentist. All three enjoyed sharing their memories of the old neighborhood team.

"The Neighborhood House had a basketball court," Mudrick said. "I'm telling you there were no seats—there was no room. If you were watching

The South Parkway basketball team during the 1930s. *From top left*: Hal Brown, Abe Pearl and Bob Mudrick (in the suit). *Middle row, left*: Jake Weinstein, Frank Riback, Milton Levenson, Lou Rotenberg. *Bottom row, left*: Joe Unkeles, Sol Siegel, Harold Mink (with the basketball), Ike Donin and Max Brell. *Courtesy Dr. Larry Mudrick.*

Larry Mudrick. *Photo by author.*

a game, you stood on the court. They had a Jewish Club called Hakoah. Eventually, the name became South Parkway. My brother was coach; everybody loved that guy."

Bob Mudrick dropped out of school and took care of his mother and five siblings after his father died. He worked at a downtown wholesale clothing company, but basketball was his passion.

Larry Mudrick remembers one incident with a now internationally famous team: "Have you heard of the Harlem Globetrotters? Abe Saperstein owned the club. He came to Portland to schedule a game with the South Parkway team. He met my brother at the Multnomah Hotel on Fourth Street. My brother said, 'We'll give you twenty-five dollars after expenses.' Abe said, 'I want the twenty-five dollars before expenses.' Bottom line: they couldn't agree and never scheduled the game."

Later, Bob Mudrick coached for the city leagues that took over the basketball scene. "They'd get tremendous crowds at the high schools; that's where they used to play." Larry Mudrick said. "They had the major

Harold Mink. *Photo by author.*

Ike Donin. *Photo by author.*

championships in Denver. Teams from all over the country came. One year, my brother's team won the championship in Portland, and he took them to Denver. They defeated the number one seed in a preliminary game."

Harold Mink still has the basketball from his own game in Denver. "It's painted white and has all our names on it," he said. "Bob Mudrick was coach. He was a super guy."

During the late 1940s, their team won the Oregon State Basketball Championship. Next stop was the Amateur Athletic Union tournament in Colorado. "We played the Peoria Caterpillars," Mink said. "They were the third seeded team, and we beat them. Next day we played the U.S. Naval Academy."

"On the East Coast, basketball players were primarily Jewish at that time," Mink continued. "When I was older and played for the Jewish Community Center we played in the YMHA [Young Men's Hebrew Association] tournament in Montreal. We came in second. The next year we won the national YMHA basketball tournament in Detroit."

Like Mudrick, Mink has a large, framed copy of the old South Parkway photo. Of course, he was a child and the others were young men. "What was I doing in the picture? Beats me," he said. "Maybe I happened to be strolling by. I lived in South Portland. My father owned a grocery on First and Porter."

"Abe Pearl was a real comedian," he said as he gazed at the photo, remembering how the players turned out. "Jake Weinstein owned a women's clothing store in Longview, Washington. Sol Segal became an attorney. Frank Riback was one of the best handball players in Oregon. He won the singles championship for I don't know how many years."

Isaac Leonard Donin (Ike) also remembers the team and especially Bob Mudrick. "He was a lovable fellow," he said. "We played in the old Neighborhood House. They had a running track around the top of the basketball court. It made it a little difficult to play, but it was fun. And we won the championship in 1935."

Donin and his family emigrated from Kiev and joined a relative in Portland shortly after his birth in 1911. "My dad was brilliant," he said. "Before you knew it, he built up stores, furniture, groceries, anything like that. He was also president of Shaarie Torah. We lived on Southwest Fifth and Grant."

The *Oregonian* named Donin an Inter-Scholastic All-Star in 1929. He played basketball for the Jewish Community Center's AZA (Aleph Zadik Aleph) team before switching to South Parkway at the Neighborhood House.

"I'll tell you a story about this," he said about his time with AZA. "They had a German Community Center across from the Jewish Community Center. We had to play ball against them. The Nazis were in force at that time. I've never played in a ballgame that was as rough from the audience. They threw things at us. And did we ever give [that team] a licking."

Donin received an athletic scholarship from the University of Oregon. "Bill Bowerman was my roommate when we traveled from one city to another playing colleges," he said, referring to the famous University of Oregon track-and-field coach. "One time I was in my office and Bill walked in. He'd started a new shoe company that Phil Knight took over. Phil's sister told me to get in on this, but I was too 'smart.' It became Nike. Anyway, we became good friends."

## A SETTLEMENT HOUSE WORKER SHINES

Ida Loewenberg (1872–1949) stands out among Portland's early leaders. Born to privilege and schooled in Europe, her mansion and servants disappeared after her father's death—but not her determination.

The Neighborhood House, 3030 Southwest Second, 1910, photographer unknown, original rendering by Doyle & Patterson Architects. *Courtesy State Historic Preservation Office.*

As director of Neighborhood House during the early twentieth-century wave of Eastern European immigration, she used her advantaged background to help the newcomers—every day for thirty-two years. Founded by the National Council of Jewish Women, the community center at 3030 Southwest Second Avenue anchored South Portland's immigrant district.

"So many groups met there," said Loewenberg's niece, Gladys Trachtenberg, in a 1973 interview with the Jewish Historical Society of Oregon, now the Oregon Jewish Museum. "Your sick benefit association, your burial society, what today we would call a health insurance society. They printed their own newspaper for a while."

Trachtenberg remembered the scene Loewenberg found when she started community work in late 1912. Like the Lower East Side of New York, the immigrants replicated the self-contained communities they had left in Europe.

"You would see Koessel and Fry's butcher shop," Trachtenberg said. "If you went on a Friday morning, you would see all the Jewish ladies going down the stairs to the basement. They would come up petting their little wild chicken and go down the street to Mr. Levine, the shochet, and have it killed."

Quite a different world than Southwest Park Avenue, where Loewenberg grew up. Born to Bavarian immigrant parents, her father, Julius, founded Merchants National Bank and Northwest Fire and Marine Insurance.

Loewenberg and sisters Zerlina and Rose attended the Episcopal St. Helen's Hall and her brother, Sidney, Bishop Scott Academy. The family spent 1890 in Europe to further the children's education.

When Julius Loewenberg returned from Europe that year, he built a mansion at the entrance to Washington Park. Fashioned after a stone castle he remembered from childhood, he furnished the thirty-two rooms with treasures from Europe. Even the servants came from the Hamburg apartment the family rented: a governess, a houseman, a groom, an upstairs maid and a cook.

However, Julius Loewenberg lost his fortune in the crash of 1897. After his 1899 death, the family sold the mansion and eventually moved to a house on Southwest Tenth Avenue. Zerlina Loewenberg became South Portland's head librarian. Ida Loewenberg became a stenographer at her brother's firm, Loewenberg and Going, until the Neighborhood House hired her in late 1912.

Loewenberg summed up her first year in the 1913–14 Head Worker's Report. "There are 28 classes including kindergarten, sewing, domestic science, manual training, gymnasium, English and religion," she wrote. "Ten paid workers and 50 volunteers help in our work to train those unaccustomed to the standards of American homes to a new and better environment and to explain the modern laws of sanitation and industry."

By 1915, her report was lamenting Portland's failure to open a community night school: "Our English department was very much crowded. At times we were hard pressed for teachers and room space. The school was the largest in the history of the work, and the quality of the students the finest." A dark spot, she reported, "is the lack of veneration on the part of our youth for the old teachings of Judaism. Their ignorance of the Bible is astounding."

Trachtenberg talked about her aunt's relationship with South Portlanders. "I am sure she knew more about their private lives and their families, for they would come running to her when anything happened for advice," she said. "She was more like a mother confessor than anything, and any problems they expected her to solve. The county hospital was across the street from the Neighborhood House. And believe me there was many a time that my aunt would have to take these people over to the hospital. They were afraid to go, and they needed hospitalization."

Loewenberg also served as secretary to the Portland Hebrew School. They held classes on the Neighborhood House's top floor. She championed the Yiddish drama group. "Yiddish literature," she wrote, "being one of the most potent agents for awakening and fostering a Jewish consciousness…we have encouraged the use of this language wherever we could."

Loewenberg furthered her own education attending the Portland School of Social Work when it opened in 1919. Part of the University of Oregon's extension services, Edward T. Devine, the nationally known director of the New York School of Philanthropy, taught her summer session. University of Oregon records show that Loewenberg studied Hebrew and social work during 1922 and 1923.

"Aunt Ida was extremely intelligent and progressive," Trachtenberg said. She remembered her aunt's inventive thinking like a children's penny bank she started and her response when donations couldn't match her vision. "My aunt was able to get money personally from the most prominent people in Portland, people like the Failing family, the Corbetts and Mr. Joseph Teal," Trachtenberg said. "These were the people who supported the Neighborhood House. They were the people my mother and aunts had grown up with. They all went to St. Helen's Hall."

A swimming pool started as Ida Loewenberg's dream. She made it happen with the help of friends. After attending a Chicago seminar, she opened one of Portland's first day camps.

"She was a lady to be reckoned with," said Frieda Cohen, who grew up in South Portland and worked for Loewenberg while attending Reed College. "She was precise but kind. She wanted things run correctly."

Cohen remembered a slender, attractive woman with straight, pulled-back hair. "She always wore a simple dress and she had pinch-nose glasses that she would take off and put on all the time. She was most interested in seeing to it that the immigrants got to be citizens."

In 1939, Ida and Zerlina Loewenberg moved to a Multnomah Village home built by Trachtenberg's parents. The South Portland Branch Library and Zerlina Loewenberg transferred to the Multnomah Station branch in 1940, according to the Multnomah County Library Association's annual report. Meanwhile, Ida Loewenberg remained the Neighborhood House director until 1945. The sisters left the Multnomah home to their niece and spent their last years at the Mallory Hotel.

Ida and Zerlina Loewenberg with their sister, Rose Goodman, her daughter, "Laddie" Goodman Trachtenberg, and children, Ida Jean and John Trachtenberg. *Courtesy John Trachtenberg.*

Ida Loewenberg explained her work in a 1931 *Oregonian* article titled "Intimate Glimpses of Portland Welfare Workers": "It has been a wonderful experience to watch through the years the development of character," she said. "Many have gone out from here into big places in life. They visit us and talk of old times when they were among those attending classes at the Neighborhood House, and they attribute a great deal of their success to Neighborhood House training."

## LOCAL STORIES FROM A FOREIGN WAR

When South Portlander Marvin Enkelis signed up for World War II, his mother got United States citizenship papers. "She didn't have to worry about who was this and how many Houses of Congress," he said. "She told the judge, 'I have two sons in the service.' He said, 'Madam, you are a citizen of the United States.'"

A fitting tribute to 2 of the 550,000 Jewish World War II service people—and best of all, both Enkelis boys came home alive. Now, as

Norman Berlant (right) and Irving Rotenberg on furlough in Liverpool, England, during World War II. *Courtesy Norman Berlant.*

1,600 World War II veterans pass on each day, Portlanders would like to salute our heroes Five local vets agreed to share their stories.

Stories like that of Enkelis and South Portlander Norman Berlant leaving the station together. "We got on the streetcar and our mothers waved goodbye," Enkelis said. "Norm went to Europe. I started in Australia, went to New Guinea and the Philippines and then to the occupation of Japan."

Enkelis became a platoon sergeant. "Nothing out of the ordinary," he said. "A lot of people lost their lives. My favorite story? I can't tell you my favorite story. But we were in Wadke Island [off the coast of New Guinea] on Yom Kippur. I went to services and here's this Catholic priest. He conducted services just as well as any rabbi."

His friend, Norman Berlant, volunteered at age eighteen and spent two years in England and France. "There were ten or twelve Jewish people in our outfit, doctors and soldiers like me," he said. "We got along fine with everyone."

Berlant worked in the station hospital registrar's office: "This was right after the invasion of France. Wounded soldiers came in every day. My job was getting all the information about them." He bumped into Portlander Irv Rotenberg and carries a photo of them on furlough together in his wallet to this day. "We went to Liverpool for about a week," he said.

A great basketball player, Rotenberg became the lead scorer in the European United States Army league. "One time after a basketball game they were having an ice cream sundae and a bomb went off nearby," his son, Kyle Rotenberg, said. "I'm sure he finished the sundae."

Harry Glickman, another South Portlander, remembers learning of Rotenberg's success. "One day we dug a foxhole," he said. "Someone came around passing out copies of the *Stars and Stripes* newspaper. That's where I read Irv Rotenberg led the Western Base Sector in scoring."

After the war, the two met up in Paris. "We somehow found a Jewish family who invited us home for potato latkes," Glickman said.

Glickman dropped out of the University of Oregon journalism school to join the army. He landed in France in November 1944 and became staff sergeant and head of a mortar squad. "I didn't know the extent of what was happening in Germany during the war," he said. "We lost a lot of family. My mother was from Wysoke in Poland."

Like Glickman, Charlotte Shwartz dropped out of the University of Oregon and joined the service during the war. "I was a little over twenty-one, and I felt I had to do something," she said. "The first place they sent me was Monticello, Arkansas, for WAC training. Then, I went to Smyrna, Tennessee. The planes I flew in were mostly cargo. My job was to dispatch them. For instance, if the weather were bad, I wouldn't let them go."

Schwartz keeps her sense of humor when remembering those years. "What did I hate about it? You certainly didn't have the comforts of home," she said. "We were in barracks with one hundred women sleeping on bunks. There was one other Jewish girl. It wasn't an issue."

Schwartz's favorite story involved the morning routine. "When the commanding officer came in, you stood at attention by your bunk," she said. "One girl couldn't keep her eyes straight ahead, so I told her to focus on something. Well, she shouted, 'Kellogg's, Ma'am!' when the officer asked for her name. She was staring at a box of cereal across the room."

Schwartz, too, was a South Portland girl. Like many, her family had moved to Irvington early on. "My father was a buyer of men's clothing at Meier and Frank," she said. "After the war, clothing was at a premium. You had to know someone to buy a suit. All of a sudden, I had a lot of boyfriends."

Finally, Herbert Newmark's role in the war certainly deserves recognition. He grew up in San Diego and moved to Portland in 1951. While a student at San Diego State during the war, a friend convinced him to join the navy.

"Preflight was just a toughening school," he said. "We had four hours of athletics a day and then four hours of ground school. Sometimes they'd even wake us in the middle of the night to look at the stars."

Newmark became a carrier-based fighter pilot in the Pacific. "We were in Leyte Gulf and Guadalcanal," he said. "Basically, our job was to escort the bombers and then go on and do close air support and help the troops on the ground."

"There was a war going on, and I signed up for it, and I never did anything unusual," he continued. "Nothing a lot of other people didn't do and do more of." Still, at a gathering of Corsair fighter pilots, they treated Newmark like a hero. "Because of you or people like you," they said, "my father is alive."

## Girlfriends Meet Up for Sorority Reunion

They have no idea how it started. But by the time they went to high school in the 1940s, Jewish girls from around the city had three sororities: K'Maia, Queen Esther's Daughters and Sub Debs. They elected officers, planned dances and shared laughs. The girls grew up together, and their friendships persisted throughout college, marriage, moves and careers.

Then turning eighty, a group of Sub Debs held a mid-July reunion in 2010. Seven out of twelve close friends remain. Some live in Portland, others came from out of state and stayed in one another's homes. It was a time for reflection, remembrance and reconnection, they said. They didn't stop talking for days.

"The big thing was the Purim and Yom Kippur Ball," Toinette Menashe said about her high school sorority years. At that time, Glen Miller and the Big Bands were king. "Loads of Jewish kids came to these dances. We had this orchestra called Joe Dardes."

Most of the girl's grandparents came from Eastern Europe and settled in the South Portland immigrant district. Girls who attended Hebrew school at the Neighborhood House could stop by and visit on their way home.

The 2010 Sub Deb reunion. *From front left*: Carol Schubach Salasky; Marilyn Krane Hasson; Raya Lippman Gladstein; Toinette Rosenberg Menashe; Edie Nudelman Bean; Francis Riback Berger; and Eve Overback Rosenfeld. *Photo by author.*

Sub Debs, 1945–46 class. The women who attended the 2010 reunion are in the front row: Raya Lippman Gladstein, far left; Toinette Rosenberg Menashe, second from left; Francis Riback Berger, fourth from left; Carol Schubach Salasky, ninth from left; Marilyn Krane Hasson, tenth from left; Edie Nudelman Bean, twelfth from left (holding a coat); and Eve Overback Rosenfeld, thirteenth from left. *Courtesy Toinette Menashe.*

Like many, Menashe's family moved to newer east side neighborhoods like Irvington, Laurelhurst and Ladd's Addition.

They met under the clock at Meier and Frank's department store and watched movies at the Orpheum or Paramount. During the summer, their families rented cabins at Seaside. Their newsletter, the *Teen Tattler*, kept everyone informed. After high school, the friends scattered.

The reunion started with lunch at the Cadillac Café in the heart of the Irvington neighborhood. Over custard French toast and other treats, conversation drifted across sixty-five years:

"We used to go to Paige's Drugstore and get Three Musketeers. You got three little pieces for a nickel."

"Did you read *Cutting for Stone*? It's extraordinary. And don't forget *The Help.*"

"During the war my mother was a block warden. We delivered buckets of sand to houses on our skates. Everyone was supposed to have sand in case their house was bombed. It was a crazy time."

"Anyone see that wonderful movie *Please Give*? It's like an old Woody Allen comedy."

"They're making a big deal about putting streetcars on the east side. We grew up with streetcars on the east side."

The women talked about grandchildren, Mah Jongg, book clubs and art classes. They asked what happened to so and so, and someone always knew. Finally, it was time to leave. They would stop outside the home where each woman grew up and take photos before dinner at the Stockpot. Tomorrow, they'd head for the beach.

"We are all different people, and our lives have taken different paths," Menashe said a few days later. "It was renewing an intense bond. We don't all see each other much, but when we do it's like no years have intervened. We pick up where we left off."

## Old South Portlanders Kibbitz After All These Years

When Mutzy Enkelis showed up, the place started hopping. Anyone could tell you that.

As his brother, Arnold, always said, "There are two Jews you refer to by their first name only. One is Mutzy and the other is Jesus."

And Mutzy did show up at the Skybox Pub and Grill (7981 Southeast Milwaukie Avenue) every Thursday along with other Old South Portland alumni. In their mid-eighties, they grew up together, went to school together and sometimes even joined the service together. They remembered old times and caught up on the new over lunch at the Sellwood neighborhood sports bar.

Although Mutzy died in September 2009, he has never been forgotten among the lunchtime crowd. This story recalls a happier time earlier that year when they all met up for sandwiches and coffee.

South Portland, as many know, was the immigrant district where Jews and Italians settled in the early 1900s. Roughly 1.5 square miles, about 6,000 Jews lived there by 1920. Portland's Italian population also surged, reaching 5,500 by 1910.

The tight ethnic community had kosher butcher shops, bakeries, synagogues and Italian delis before a series of highway projects cut it to shreds. By the time the 1960s Urban Renewal project razed fifty-four blocks,

Marvin (Mutzy) Enkelis (front left) and Judge Tony Casciato (front right) at the weekly reunion of Old South Portland residents. *Photo by author.*

many immigrant families had left for more prestigious neighborhoods, like Laurelhurst and Irvington.

That day, the waitress had coffee ready as small groups filtered in and joined the long reserved table.

"There is a distinction between south South Portland and upper South Portland," Mutzy said over his Rueben sandwich.

"South Portland Heights," someone snarled.

North (upper) South Portlanders lived somewhere north of Southwest Lincoln Street, attended Shattuck School and played basketball at B'nai B'rith on Southwest Thirteenth Avenue. South South Portlanders went to Failing School and the Neighborhood House, where everyone met for Hebrew school. Several at the table also enjoyed the Manley Community Center. Run by the Women's Home Missionary Society, it moved from Southwest First Avenue and Caruthers Street next to Failing School in 1929.

"Hi, Shamos," Arnold Enkelis said as former police detective Al Vigna sat down. Everyone and everything in South Portland had a nickname. Arnold, in fact, was better known as "Teta," leftover from his toddler days when he couldn't pronounce streetcar.

"We had one guy named Shagitz LaGrande," Mutzy said, in another reference to nicknames. "Shagitz made a lot of money."

The Orthodox immigrants relied on young Italians like Willy LaGrande for help with forbidden chores over Shabbas. They often lived around Duniway Park, once a large hole in the ground. The city filled the gulch with garbage dumped from trucks throughout the west side, turning it into the Children's Park, according to *Oregonian* articles. Some say that even today, lighting a match in the vicinity could cause an explosion.

"Before the days of Fred Meyer, we'd go to Mink's for sunflower seeds," Vigna said. "He'd measure them out in a shot glass."

"How many groceries did we have in South Portland?" Mutzy asked, and everyone started counting: "Shneiderman's, Korsun's, Calistro and Halperin's…"

"Tony had a pacemaker put in," someone interrupted. "He still plays slow pitch in the summer. Remember those softball games?"

Meanwhile, Judge Casciato, waiting quietly for his soup, modeled an origami boat from lottery tickets. "All the Jewish ladies seemed to have singsong voices," he said. Although his mother spoke Italian and Mutzy's Yiddish, communication, they said, worked just fine.

"The judge is good," Teta whispered. "He married us all for free."

Talk went on another hour. "Dave was quite a guy," a gentleman recalled. "I used to see him at the Captain's Bar. His cigarette ash fell in his drink, and he finished it anyway."

"The Lincoln Theater—we'd see a couple features and a cartoon," Vigna said. "Like Jackie Cooper. And Mrs. Carlin played the organ."

"The first talkie was at the Grant Street Theater," Teta chimed in.

"The stories here are told and retold," another whispered. "The guys here know them by heart."

Finally, they said goodbye. They would see one another same time same place next week. "We used to have big reunions once a year," Mutzy said as he rose to leave. "Three to four hundred people came. We had them at the Neighbors of Woodcraft Hall. We had the biggest dance bands in the city; there was food galore from 7:00 p.m. until midnight. But then it got to be too much of a chore."

"Nobody had money, and we were so close," Teta added, reflecting on the old neighborhood. "We always say: there will never be another South Portland."

*Part III*

# Our Institutions

When Jews arrive, Jewish institutions follow, often beginning with a burial ground. The Mount Sinai Cemetery Association may have been the first Jewish institution in Oregon. Incorporated in 1856, its administrators purchased land in what coincidentally became the South Portland immigrant district. Synagogues followed. Eight men founded Congregation Beth Israel in 1858. By December 1893, the *American Hebrew News* listed three synagogues, along with the First Hebrew Benevolent Association, Sisters of Israel, Judith Montefiore Society and Jewish Literary Society.

The arrival of Eastern European Jews brought new institutions. The National Council of Jewish Women, Portland Section, started its sewing school in 1897. It grew into the Neighborhood House on Southwest Second Avenue, the core of the immigrant community. The Ladies Free Loan Society offered interest-free credit, and Bikur Cholim took care of the sick. Gevurtz Hall on Gibbs Street provided a venue for Jewish events.

Since 1920, the Jewish Federation of Greater Portland has been the central planning, coordinating and fundraising body for many local and international institutions. Programs include elder care, rescue, relief, education, a Jewish newspaper and much more. This chapter gives a history and firsthand look at some of Portland's federated and nonfederated associations. M'chayil el choyil—may you go from strength to strength.

*Above*: Rose City Lodge meeting. Nina Weinstein's father, George Weinstein, is in the second row, center. *Courtesy Nina Weinstein.*

*Right*: H.I. and Braina Chernichowsky at a dinner given by the Portland Jewish community in his honor, 1953. *Courtesy Marcia Ketzlach Gale.*

The Ramblers (Right, Ambition, Merit, Benevolence, Love, Energy, Religion, Service) at the B'nai B'rith Center in 1921. *Courtesy Dr. Larry Mudrick.*

# A SHORT HISTORY OF THE JEWISH FEDERATION OF GREATER PORTLAND

When Charlie Schiffman joined the Jewish Federation of Greater Portland (JFGP) in 1987, he found a friendly, manageable city. "They described a small, cohesive Jewish community with a few synagogues," he said, remembering recruitment literature. Not quite the 45,700 Jews, fourteen synagogues and potpourri of viewpoints found today. Not like in 2010, when about half of Portland's Jews were not on the list of any organization, synagogue or newspaper connected with the established Jewish community, according to the recent JFGP survey.

"We're integrated [into society], which is wonderful," said Schiffman, who retired on June 30, 2010. "Jews can go anywhere and do anything. But people are still unemployed, ill or need elderly care. There are pockets of poverty overseas, as well as in the States. We have an obligation to play a role in providing that support. The federation's greatest challenge is explaining the urgency of what we do."

In fact, shifting challenges have been part of the scene since the federation's inception in 1919. The decades of federation history tell the story of our community's changing times. While today's amorphous, diversified population differs from the insular society our grandparents knew, the JFGP's adaptation and response have remained constant throughout the years.

Charles R. Schiffman. *Courtesy Charles R. Schiffman.*

When the Federated Jewish Societies of Portland, as the JFGP was first called, was formed in 1919, local needs loomed large. The *American Jewish Yearbook* set Portland's Jewish population at nine thousand. Most lived in the South Portland immigrant district.

"Amongst the crying needs are those of orphans, the aged, the sick, poor and social service amongst adolescents," reported Portland's Jewish newspaper, the *Scribe*. "The Federation should be able to provide the funds and the guidance." The thirteen original federation agencies included the South Portland Benevolent Society, Portland Hebrew Free School and the Neighborhood House.

Marc N. Blattner. *Courtesy Paul Haist/*Jewish Review.

The Tenth Annual Northwest Conclave of Aleph Zadik Aleph in front of the B'nai B'rith Center. *Courtesy Dr. Larry Mudrick.*

During the Depression, JFGP executive secretary Julia Swett summed up the organization's role in a September 30, 1931 *Oregonian* article: "Individuals come to us with their troubles…We must do what we can to alleviate their suffering, for many are suffering these days." In a statement eerily similar to the federation experience today, she added, "Many who have never found it necessary to ask for agency aid are doing so now on account of the unemployment situation."

The focus changed in 1936 when the Oregon Jewish Welfare Fund's first campaign ran "in response to Nuremberg laws depriving Jews of their citizenship and rights." Originally chartered to train and transport Jews and other refugees to Palestine, OJWF expanded to include local, national and international causes not covered by the Federated Jewish Societies of Portland. The two organizations ran in parallel until 1956, when they merged to become the Jewish Welfare Federation of Portland. Later, the name changed to today's Jewish Federation of Greater Portland.

During the 1940s, organization agencies helped the war effort. The Oregon Émigré Committee united concentration camp survivors with Portland relatives. The Jewish Community Center formed the army and navy hospitality committee. When attention shifted to immigrants pouring into Israel, the JCC organized collection drives.

By 1951, the largest portion of the Federated Jewish Societies of Portland's budget went toward support of nonsectarian programs for

children and families at the Neighborhood House and JCC, according to the *Oregonian*. At the same time, the OJWF supported forty-six overseas, national and local organizations.

In September 1967, the *Jewish Review* headlined "Portland Responds to Emergency." The Israel Emergency Campaign following the Arab-Israeli War brought "new highs in giving." Soon, Soviet Jewish immigration became the top priority. The federation-sponsored Jewish Family and Child Service handled Russian settlement coordination.

"Portland was a leader in the number of [Soviet] families we took in," said Laurie Rogoway, now JFGP associate executive vice-president. "We had rallies and marches. We spent years protesting, and once the gates opened, we shifted resources into settling people here or in Israel. It took millions of dollars, and the community rose to the occasion."

Throughout the years, the key to the federation's effectiveness, Rogoway said, is following through on promises. "We will always have responsibility for raising funds for emergencies like Katrina and Haiti and for the most vulnerable members of our community," she said. "We're involved in the JCC, the Portland Jewish Academy and the Oregon Jewish Museum. We've added the Florence Melton Adult Mini School, Maimonides Jewish Day School and Portland Hillel to our list of supported agencies. Jewish education and youth are primary."

The JFGP's new executive director, Marc Blattner, agreed. "We want to continue our historic mission of enhancing Jewish life here, in Israel and overseas while understanding the new realities of the Portland Jewish community," he said. "We have to look at outreach initiatives and serve a community that is growing. People involve themselves in the Jewish community in traditional avenues and in nontraditional avenues. We have to be open to that."

Blattner sees a bright future. "As we celebrate the accomplishments of the past ninety years, I am most interested in where federation will be at one hundred," he said. "We have an opportunity to do great things over the coming ten years to make Portland the premier Jewish community in North America and the premier destination for Jewish families. That's the goal. I'm looking forward to working with the Jewish and non-Jewish community and making things better. I want this to be a great place for my kids for generations to come."

FEDERATION TIMELINE

| | |
|---|---|
| 1919 | The JFGP started when a group from the Portland Committee on Relief of Jewish War Sufferers united local Jewish agencies. They named the new organization Federated Jewish Societies of Portland and elected Ben Selling president. The original agencies were the First Hebrew Benevolent Society, Jewish Relief Society, Jewish Women's Sewing Society, Jewish Women's Benevolent Society, Sisters of Israel Benevolent Society, Bikur Cholim Aid Society, First Voliner Benefit Society, Ahavath Achim Society, South Portland Benevolent Society, Jewish Women's Endeavor Society, B'nai B'rith Building Association, Portland Hebrew Free School and the Neighborhood House. Affiliated agencies changed over the years. |
| 1920 | After the first campaign in 1920, the Federated Jewish Societies of Portland received money through the Community Chest. FJSP agencies had Community |

| | |
|---|---|
| | Chest representatives. For example, in 1922 Max Hirsch represented the American Jewish Relief Society, Julia Swett the B'nai B'rith Building Association and Ben Selling the First Hebrew Benevolent Society. |
| 1927 | The local newspaper, the *Scribe, A Record of Jewish Life and Thought* reported a new fund for nonlocal charities: "There comes annually to Portland a great many solicitors for contributions, representing Jewish relief agencies situated outside of this city and state... In a great measure this interferes with our local drives for the Community Chest." A federation committee organized a fund for nonlocal charities. |
| 1936 | The *Oregonian* announced the formation of the Oregon Jewish Welfare Fund under the headline "Jewry Hastens Welfare Drive": "The future for Jews in Germany is anything but bright and conditions for Semites in the Nazi-ruled country will become worse after the 1936 Olympic Games." Julius Meier led the campaign that raised funds to train and transport German Jews to Palestine. |
| 1936–55 | The Federated Jewish Societies of Portland and the Oregon Jewish Welfare Fund ran in parallel. In 1950, the FJSP agencies were the Jewish Community Center, Neighborhood House, Home for the Aged, Family and Child Services and Relief and Benevolent Society. The OJWF's 1947 annual report listed local organizations including the Council of Jewish Women, Jewish Educational Association, Oregon Émigré Committee and Women's Division of the National Jewish Welfare Board. The Jewish Labor Committee, National Farm School, American Committee for Relief of Yemenite |

| | |
|---|---|
| | Jews, and the United Jewish Appeal were among the national and overseas organizations. |
| 1956 | *Scribe* editorials advocated an FJSP and OJWF merger since the early 1950s. In 1956, the two organizations joined to become the Jewish Welfare Federation of Portland and elected Arthur A. Goldsmith as the first president. Today, the organization is called the Jewish Federation of Greater Portland. |

FEDERATION LEADERSHIP

*Executive Directors*

| | |
|---|---|
| 1920 | Isaac C. Swett (died September 19, 1921) |
| 1921 to 1946 | Julia Swett |
| 1947 to 1963 | Milton D. Goldsmith |
| 1964 to 1966 | Clifford Josephson |
| 1967 to 1977 | Morris A. Stein |
| 1977 to 1982 | David Roberts |
| 1982 to 1983 | Bob Tropp, acting executive director |
| 1983 to 1986 | Murray N. Schneier |
| 1987 | Laurie Rogoway, acting executive director |
| 1988 to 2010 | Charles R. Schiffman |
| September 1, 2010 | Marc N. Blattner |

*Presidents*

Ben Selling was the first president of the Federated Jewish Societies of Portland and held that post until 1930. A partial list of other presidents includes Nathan Strauss and Julius L. Meier.

Executive Director Morris Stein with Rosemary Rosenfeld, Ruth Saltzman and Hal Saltzman. *Courtesy Ruth Saltzman.*

Between 1936 and 1955, the Federated Jewish Societies of Portland (FJSP) and Oregon Jewish Welfare Fund (OJWF) ran in parallel, often with the same executive director. FJSP presidents included Max Hirsch, Harold Miller, Samuel B. Weinstein and Justin Reinhardt.

OJWF presidents included Julius L. Meier, S. Mason Ehrman, Abe Eugene Rosenberg, Julius Zell, Harry A. Herzog, Abe Leo Cohn, Louis Gevurtz, Ben Rosenfeld, William Tannenbaum, Alfred Davis and Jack Olds.

In 1956, the FJSP and OJWF united to become the Jewish Welfare Federation of Portland. The name changed to the Jewish Federation of Portland in 1980 and to the Jewish Federation of Greater Portland in 2005. The following is a list of federation presidents in order of service since 1956:

Arthur A. Goldsmith
Jack W. Olds
David W. Cohn

Henry Blauer
Hershal M. Tanzer
Harold H. Saltzman
James A. Meyer
Kurt Hamburger
Arden E. Shenker
Stanley G. Marcus
Jonathan Newman
Phil Blank
Harold Pollin
Dr. Leonard Goldberg
Stanley D. Geffen
Steve Rosenberg
Elizabeth Menashe
Paul Schlesinger
Gayle Romain
Priscilla Kostiner
Rob Shlachter
N. Dickson (Dick) Davis
Bob Philip
Gersham Goldstein

## A SHORT HISTORY OF PORTLAND SYNAGOGUES

A city's Jewish institutions often start with burial grounds. Synagogues follow. Oregon celebrated its first Jewish wedding at Beth Israel in 1858. Then a loft upstairs from a livery stable, the congregation now worships in one of Portland's most beautiful buildings.

This overview of today's Portland synagogues shows the history of immigration to the area and the changing times. The recent proliferation of congregations reflects the eclectic and geographically dispersed community. The population of 120 Jews out of 2,874 in 1860 became 45,700 Jews out of 583,776 by 2010.

Congregation Shaarie Torah, Southwest First Avenue and Hall Street, 1906. *Courtesy Portland Development Commission.*

## *1856: The Mount Sinai Cemetery Association*

The Mount Sinai Cemetery Association may be Oregon's first Jewish institution. Early Portland maps place it near what is now the Ross Island Bridge entrance. Coincidentally, this area became the South Portland Jewish and Italian immigrant district.

Congregation Beth Israel absorbed the association in 1862, but the history is sketchy. A December 9, 1885 *Morning Oregonian* article reported that the congregation appealed when the "laying out of Corbett Street… cut off part of the old Jewish cemetery," and they were "assessed $400 for the removal of graves." City contractors exhumed the bodies and reburied them in the new grounds, according to an 1887 *Oregonian* article on early cemeteries. Today Beth Israel's Cemetery on Southwest Taylor's Ferry Road includes relocated old graves.

## *1858: Congregation Beth Israel, Rabbi Michael Z. Cahana, Reform*

The first congregation west of the Rockies and north of California, Congregation Beth Israel started above a livery stable on First Avenue.

On August 24, 1861, the *Weekly Oregonian* published a letter from Beth Israel secretary Ben Norden to Reverend Elkan Cohn of San Francisco thanking him for consecrating their new building. Located on Southwest Fifth Avenue and Oak Street, the Gothic-style structure cost $4,500 and seated two hundred.

Many of the city's earliest Jewish settlers belonged to Beth Israel. Most originally came from Germany, and several were among the city's leading businessmen and politicians. They used the *Minhag Ashkenaz*, an Orthodox prayer book that had German translations opposite the Hebrew. A movement of some congregants toward Reform Judaism began in 1873. Beth Israel joined the Union of American Hebrew Congregations in 1879.

Arson destroyed Beth Israel's second synagogue on Southwest Twelfth Avenue and Main Street in 1923. The current structure on Northwest Flanders Street is among the finest examples of Byzantine architecture in the Northwest.

### *1869: Congregation Neveh Shalom, Rabbi Daniel Isaak, Rabbi Bradley Greenstein, Conservative*

Congregation Neveh Shalom's roots date back to 1869, when Prussian immigrants founded Ahavai Shalom, the "Polisha Shul." In 1961, Ahavai Shalom and Neveh Tzedek Talmud Torah combined to become Neveh Shalom. At that time, the Jewish population shifted from east side neighborhoods to Southwest Portland around Hillsdale. Neveh Shalom built their synagogue in the heart of the community's new location.

Toinette Menashe's grandparents belonged to Neveh Tzedek Talmud Torah. She met her husband in kindergarten at Ahavai Shalom. "My father was president of Ahavai Shalom, and my uncle was president of Neveh Tzedek," she said. Her family helped with the merger negotiations.

Menashe remembered the succession of buildings, first at Park Avenue ("My husband and I were the last wedding there") and then at Southwest Thirteenth Avenue ("We were still in the building when the roof caved in"). When Neveh Shalom moved to Southwest Portland, she knew all had worked out for the best. "I especially loved the fact that we had religious school classrooms and, at long last, a wonderful library," she said. Like other congregants, she enjoys the 2008 expansion. "It's a huge change—a 250-seat chapel, wonderful new offices and classrooms. We're close to everything. You feel a nucleus here."

### *1902: Congregation Shaarie Torah, Rabbi Arthur Zuckerman, Independent Contemporary*

When Eastern European immigrants founded the Northwest's first Orthodox congregation, they met in a downtown hall. By 1905, they'd purchased and moved a Presbyterian church to Southwest First. "It was a narrow building with a basement called a social hall," said longtime congregant Milt Carl. "We called Rabbi Fain the Royta Rov because he had a red beard."

Carl became a Bar Mitzvah in 1938. "Nowadays it's like a wedding. In those days we got a fountain pen that leaked," he said. "They finally got

Esther Chernichowsky's wedding, February 9, 1947, at the Neighbors of Woodcraft Hall in Portland. *Seated from left*: Mendel Baronsky, Norman Ketzlach, Esther Chernichowsky Ketzlach, H.I. Chernichowsky, Rabbi Joseph Fain and Rabbi Philip Kleinman. *Standing*: Sheldon Steinberg and Frieda Gass Cohen. *Courtesy Marcia Ketzlach Gale.*

a little less traditional—some members insisted their wives sit with them." Urban Renewal and freeway construction forced two relocations. They dedicated the Northwest Twenty-fifth Avenue building in 1965. "The first social event," Carl said, "was my parent's fiftieth anniversary."

### *1912: Congregation Kesser Israel, Rabbi Kenneth Brodkin, Orthodox*

Kesser Israel's archivist Sura Rubenstein wrote this history of the congregation: "Congregation Kesser Israel was founded in the heart of historic Old South Portland by a group of Eastern European immigrants and until 2006 occupied the 'Meade Street Shul,' a former Baptist church on Southwest Meade Street. Peddler Oscar Kirshner, who fled Russia to escape service in the Czar's army, served as president for more than 40 years, followed in the mid-1960s by Holocaust survivor Barry Brown. Since its move to Southwest Capitol Highway in 2007, the congregation has experienced a renaissance as more young families move to the area."

Interior of Kesser Israel Synagogue at Southwest Meade Street. *Courtesy Elie Bulka, Oolite Photography.*

### *1916: Congregation Ahavath Achim, Sephardic*

According to former president Richard Matza, Ahavath Achim started when ten Portland men got together for the 1916 High Holiday services. Most early congregants were immigrants from Turkey or Rhodes and lived in the Old South Portland neighborhood. "In this congregation, we had people who shined shoes, had fruit and vegetable markets, sold fish and had taverns," Matza said. "They were small business people, and most of them eked a living out that way." Today, the beehive-shaped synagogue on Barbur Boulevard includes Persian, Israeli, Moroccan and Yemenite families, among others. Regarding affiliation, Matza described Sephardic Judaism as "a big tent that allows everybody to come in. We observe in the same way that our ancestors observed."

### *1978: Havurah Shalom, Rabbi Joseph Wolf, Reconstructionist*

Margie Rosenthal was part of the small group who founded the new congregation. "Most of us were in our early thirties, and we all had young kids," she said. They wanted a participatory, informal experience where parents taught religious school and "everyone sang and everyone learned." It was and is, she explained, "an opportunity to join in."

### *1984: Congregation Bais Menachem, Rabbi Motti Wilhelm, Chabad*

When Rabbi Moshe Wilhelm celebrated his fiftieth birthday, cards poured in from around the world. He came to Oregon from his post in Australia at the direction of the late Lubavitcher Rebbe Menachem M. Schneerson. "My father gave the congregation leadership to me as his role expanded," said his son, Motti Wilhelm. Today, Rabbi Moshe Wilhelm serves as director of Chabad Oregon. This includes nine regional centers and ten full-time rabbis.

### *1984: Women's Tefillah*

Women's Tefillah groups grew out of the Orthodox community, explained Portland cofounder Erica Goldman. "There was a desire to have a traditional service where women could participate." The Portland group meets once a month, uses a traditional prayer book and enjoys melody and singing. "All women and girls are welcome," Goldman said. "It's particularly lovely to see the girls come of age and take their place in the community."

### *1989: Congregation Kol Ami, Rabbi Elizabeth Dunsker, Reform*

When the Jewish Community Association of Southwest Washington started in 1989, most members belonged to Portland congregations. As the group grew, the members needed something closer to home. They became a liberal, egalitarian and inclusive congregation in 1998, changed their name to Kol Ami in 2001 and affiliated with the Union of Reform Judaism in 2004.

"From the beginning, it has been the center of Jewish life in Clark County," said former president Douglas Green. In 2007, an anonymous donor gave the congregation $6 million to build a new synagogue, which will open in 2011. "It's not just where people live," Green said. "The leadership part is to peer into the future and hopefully raise the bar."

### *1991: Congregation P'nai Or, Rabbi David Zaslow (Interim), Jewish Renewal*

Anne LeVant Prahl joined P'nai Or when it was three months old. "It began with eight or ten couples who had known Aryeh Hirshfield when he lived in Portland—before he was a rabbi," she said. After Hirshfield studied with Jewish Renewal founder Rabbi Zalman Schachter-Shalomi, he returned to Oregon and served an Ashland congregation. The couples invited him to teach and lead a prayer group in Portland once a month.

"It grew quickly—within two years it was drawing more than sixty people to Friday night services," Prahl said. Hirshfield eventually moved to Portland, and the congregation rented space at Portland churches and Portland State University. Today, they meet at St. Mark Presbyterian Church in Southwest Portland. Aryeh Hirshfield died on January 7, 2009.

### *1992: Congregation Beit Haverim, Rabbi Alan Berg, Reform*

When West Linn families decided that their children's Jewish education should be close to home, they formed Jewish Education of West Linn. It became the

South Metro Jewish Community. Under Rabbi Larry Halpern's direction, the name changed to South Metro Congregation, and they affiliated with the Union for Reform Judaism. In 2007, they adopted their Hebrew name, Beit Haverim, which means "House of Friends." "It is a community that started and has maintained itself based on friendship," said former president Steve Bilow. "It's based on people being there for each other."

### *1992: East Side Kehila*

In 1992, a group of east side Jews needed something close to home. At that time, all of Portland's Jewish institutions were west of the Willamette River. Forty people attended the first meeting. They called themselves the Eastside Jewish Community of Portland.

At first, they met for Shabbat dinner at local restaurants. The first Shabbat service in 1997 drew such enthusiasm that they continued them every month. Organizers realized that east side Jews needed a social and religious connection where they lived, especially newcomers, the elderly and the unaffiliated.

The Jewish Federation of Greater Portland agreed and provided grants in 2000 and 2001. This strengthened the congregation and their connection to other Portland institutions.

### *1993: Congregation Kol Shalom, Community for Humanistic Judaism*

"I valued connections to the Jewish community and wanted to celebrate Judaism but was not comfortable with a theistic approach," said Kol Shalom's founder Jane Goldhamer. "We are not rigidly doctrinaire. Many [members] say they are agnostic, some believe in God. The important thing is our values and our behavior."

Congregation Kol Shalom offers Sunday school through Bar and Bat Mitzvah, Yiddish and other classes and performs intercultural weddings in which "one person comes from a Jewish background and one doesn't."

### *2001: Congregation Tefillat Emet, Cantor Aaron Vitells*

Dina Feuer was among a small group who envisioned a different kind of shul. "No dues, no organization—just come in and pray," she said. Then called the Egalitarian Shul, they had no rabbi or committees. "You didn't have to become a member. In the beginnings in America, there were storefront shuls. That's what we wanted to create, and we did."

The congregation met at the Mittleman Jewish Community Center and then at the Rose Schnitzer Chapel. "We had well-attended Rosh Hashanah and Yom Kippur services," Feuer said. "By word of mouth, we could have two hundred to three hundred people." After about eight years, the leadership dispersed, and the shul temporarily disbanded.

In 2010, three hundred people turned out for a community Yom Kippur service led by Cantor Aaron Vitells. He announced the shul had reemerged under the name Tefillat Emet.

### *2002: Congregation Shir Tikvah, Rabbi Ariel Stone, Reform*

According to 2011 Membership Co-Chair Edward Hershey, Shir Tikvah started with fifteen people looking for an intimate Jewish experience. "They were very taken by a former assistant rabbi at Beth Israel," he said. They contacted Rabbi Ariel Stone in Israel and asked if she would return to Portland to work with them on a new congregation. Today Shir Tikvah holds services at the Bridgeport Community Church in Northeast Portland.

### *2006: Beit Midrash Eitz Chaim*

Rabbi Kim Rosen got the idea for Beit Midrash Eitz Chaim while attending the Shalom Hartman Institute in Jerusalem. "Every summer rabbis from the different movements come together," she said. "Many adults in our community want to study our sacred text in depth in an egalitarian environment. It is in addition to all the learning they're doing at synagogue."

### *2006: Portland Kollel*

"We are not a synagogue. We may be a community," said Rabbi Tzvi Fischer about Portland Kollel. "Our focus is to build community sense through Torah study and day-to-day Jewish living." According to Fischer, the concept of community kollels started thirty to forty years ago. In 2010, the United States had forty. The local group began when Seattle's eighteen-year-old kollel decided to expand.

Fischer emphasized that all are welcome. "Many of the people who associate with us are not affiliated at all," he said. "Some are intermarried, some are Orthodox, some are Reform, some are Humanist. Hundreds of people come to our classes and functions."

### *2007: Congregation Beit Yosef, Rabbi Shlomo Truzman, Sephardic*

Beit Yosef started with a group of Portlanders who wanted a Sephardic Mizrachi synagogue, said Rabbi Shlomo Truzman. After meeting in private homes for a year, they turned a Northwest space into a makeshift shul. When a storefront next to the Jewish Federation of Greater Portland opened, they moved in. "Those lamps you see—the decorations were all brought from Morocco," Truzman said. "A member of our congregation donated them when he moved to California."

Rabbi Truzman is also originally from Morocco, or rather the Spanish protectorate Melilla near the Mediterranean coast. "We do use some Ladino in services," he said. "The bulk of our congregation is Eastern European. We attract people from all walks of life."

## The 1930s: May You Live in Interesting Times

The Chinese curse "May you live in interesting times" applies to 1930s Jewish Portland. The Depression, followed by the rise of Nazism, dominated the scene. Zionism and the evacuation of European Jews to Palestine formed the backbone of local aid efforts. Smaller groups formed, like ICOR, an organization that promoted a Jewish homeland in Siberia (see textbox).

#### Association for Jewish Colonization in the Soviet Union (ICOR)

In 1934, the Soviet government established a Jewish homeland in Siberia. Officially called the Jewish Autonomous Region (JAR), many referred to it by the area's capital city, Birobidzhan.

About eighteen thousand Jews moved to the JAR from other parts of Russia and from Lithuania, Argentina and the United States. The Association for Jewish Colonization in the Soviet Union (ICOR) promoted awareness and raised funds for the project. One hundred ICOR chapters were organized throughout the United States.

According to *Oregonian* newspaper accounts, the Portland chapter of ICOR met regularly during the mid-1930s. Members held meetings at the Linath Hazedek Synagogue, B'nai B'rith and the Neighborhood House. A December 1933 *Oregonian* article titled "Jewish Situation Studied" reported, "The Portland ICOR organization, being an international association for assisting Jewish pioneers in Biro Bidjan, Jewish colonization project in Soviet Russia, discussed the world Jewish situation and the colony at a recent mass meeting. The session was well attended, according to the announcement, and many of those present enrolled for membership."

ICOR held picnics and annual balls. In 1934, Linath Hazedek exhibited "the first machinery which is to be sent from Portland to the Jewish pioneers in Biro Bidjan."

The Federated Jewish Societies of Portland started the decade with its annual report. Executive Secretary Julia Swett commented on economic stress and reduced funds. Still, the Jewish Service Association helped 170 families. The Jewish Relief and South Portland Benevolent Societies provided meals and lodging to single men. Portland's Hebrew school "kept abreast of the modern educational methods" as its alumni association met for advanced Hebrew language and literature classes.

Unemployment struck the Jewish community along with other Portlanders. From a population of 11,000 Jews in 1930 came a steady decline to about 7,128 in 1946. The federation established the Opportunity Bake Shop and held bridge parties for its support. Designed to employ women with no other means, the bakeshop idea started with pickle-making and progressed to noodles. Meanwhile, the B'nai B'rith Center

Elizabeth Blane (child with blond braids) and her family escaped Austria and moved to a farm in Tigard, photo circa 1938. *Photo by Ralph Vincent, courtesy Elizabeth Blane.*

and Neighborhood House reduced expenses by merging programs and avoiding duplication.

By 1933, chilling reports arrived from Germany. Dr. Jonah Wise, chairman of the Joint Distribution Committee campaign, pleaded for assistance in an open letter to Portland's Jewish newspaper, the *Scribe*. The paper headlined "Reichstag Adopts Jew Laws Branding Jews as Inferior Race," "Reich School Degree in Effect" and "Nazis Launch New Drive to Dejudaise Legal and Economic Sciences." Warnings became more dire as months and years went by.

The Portland Zionist and Hadassah organizations promoted Zionism and aid to German Jews. In 1933, Harry Mittleman chaired the Palestine Appeal Campaign. The Jewish Welfare Fund focused on transporting Jews and other refugees to Palestine. "The future for Jews in Germany is anything but bright," a 1936 campaign announcement said. "Conditions for Semites in the Nazi-ruled country will become worse after the 1936 Olympic Games."

On Christmas 1938, the *Oregonian* carried an article about refugees in Portland. "Resettlement of Jewish refugees in this country has been accomplished almost entirely by the voluntary efforts of Jewish organizations," it noted. By this time, Jews could not leave Germany with money and could not enter the United States without it. Federation president Max Hirsch led the Oregon Émigré Committee, which handled Portland's one hundred or so refugees. The committee planned two farm projects, one in Grants Pass and the other in the Willamette Valley.

Almost in answer to the 1938 article, an April 1939 story titled "Ja, We Are Happy" gave an idealized account of Jewish refugees who settled on a Tigard farm. The two young cousins portrayed in the article, Elizabeth Kubin Blane and Karl Kubin, still live in Portland.

"I landed at Christmastime 1938 and crossed the United States in early '39," said Kubin, who left Austria at age nine. "In the old country, my father was a horse dealer, but we ended up living on the Cedarbrook Dairy. The name of the place was Cipole, for all the onion farmers out there…We milked forty cows and hauled milk every day. I worked at a neighbor's place weeding onions. My Aunt Helen baked the old-fashioned round loaves, and she had her egg business. We went to a two-room school. There were three of us in each class."

His cousin, Blane, remembered a dozen people living on the farm. "We all lived in one house, but every family had a room," she said. "None of them were farmers in any way, shape or form…They had come down in life so much. We were solid middle-class business people in Europe. We had a live-in maid. [The German authorities] took your savings accounts, insurance policies; they stole everything we had. Everyone on the farm was traumatized."

Although affidavits to the United States were next to impossible to obtain, influential Portland relatives pulled strings. Gretel and Egon Ullman arrived earlier and lived in Corvallis, where he taught at Portland State. They dealt directly with Max Hirsch and Governor Charles Martin. "Without Aunt Gretel's connections," Blane said, "we never would have got out."

### Growing Up in Depression-era Portland

Depression-era Portland doesn't seem so long ago to those who lived through those troubled years. Dr. Daniel Labby and Nina Weinstein offered to share their recollections.

Labby was born in South Portland to immigrant parents who met at Woodbine, New Jersey, a community founded by the Baron de Hirsch Fund to help immigrant Jews. His grandfather served as Shammos at Congregation Shaarie Torah, and his father became a dentist. Despite the family's relative affluence, the Depression brought hard times:

> *In 1930, I was a teen trying to get money together for college. I walked the streets of Portland along with other teens. If I wanted lunch, I'd ask a restaurant if I could clear dishes for a meal.*
>
> *The shoe stores let you stand in line, and if other salesmen were busy you could take a customer. Many times, I'd wait for my turn, and it would never come. The fashion bootery paid me to color pumps to match the girls' gowns. I gave out balloons to children on Saturday at a children's shoe store.*
>
> *By ten or eleven, I was selling newspapers on the streets. During the Rose Festival Parade, you'd sell papers for people to put on their heads if it were raining. Or the Yamhill Market would give us apple boxes, and you'd sell them to people watching the parade.*
>
> *At Grant High, I added my free period to my lunch period and worked in the cafeteria for three years. I had a business on the side. If you handed papers to the teacher with a manila cover, that gave you some points. I decorated manila covers with art figures. If they were writing about Shakespeare, I'd draw Shakespeare.*

When Nina Weinstein's parents emigrated from Ukraine, they discovered that the streets of America were "definitely not paved with gold." She grew up on Corbett Avenue:

Nina Weinstein's mother, Bluma Dypchok, in Russia. *Courtesy Nina Weinstein.*

*There was a men's-only camp under the Ross Island Bridge. They'd knock on my mother's door, and she'd say, "Go around in back." It was bad enough they had to ask. She didn't want to shame them by making them eat at the front door.*

*She always had bread, butter and coffee—her gorgeous Challah!—and would apologize that was all she could give them. My mother had a wood stove, so usually the men chopped a little wood for their meal.*

*It was right after my father died. With her meager income, my mother had a pishka, and every Friday a coin went in. Once a year, a man with a black hat would come and pry the pishka off the wall. He was from whatever organization the blue box was from. Every Jewish home had a blue box.*

## The *Jewish Review*'s Early Years

Portland in 1959 was not the scene we know today. Not according to a 1957 survey taken by the Jewish Welfare Federation of Portland, now known as the Jewish Federation of Greater Portland. Out of a population of 570,000, it said, 7,832 were Jews. The majority lived in the Northeast and Southwest, almost half were self-employed, 68 percent belonged to a synagogue and 46 percent were foreign-born.

The JWFP decided that the city needed a Jewish newspaper. Since the 1940s, federations around the country sponsored them. Portland's last publication, the *Scribe*, stopped printing in 1953. The first issue of the *Jewish Review* ran on January 1, 1959.

Ben Padrow, a Portland State University speech professor, became the volunteer editor. He published the eight-page newspaper six times a year.

Along with serving as the *Jewish Review*'s first editor, Ben Padrow (seated, far right) taught speech at Portland State University and coached the 1965 College Bowl team. *Courtesy Jim Turner, PSU Office of Alumni Relations.*

"This paper will seek to reflect the crazy-quilt pattern of a bewildering and swiftly changing world—and still try to remain close to the Jewish Community which it serves," he wrote in issue number one. "We shall function as a free newspaper—devoted to the conscience of the Jewish community and serving to unify all."

The first issue reviewed *Only in America* by Harry Golden, provided a recipe for gefilte fish and announced the Jewish Community Center Players performance of *The Crucible*. The two-column calendar offered adult education Hebrew classes along with synagogue, JWFP and social events. Judge Gus Solomon, the paper noted, had formed a local branch of the American Jewish Congress with goals of removing Jewish quotas in colleges and enacting fair employment legislation.

Advertising started in 1960 with Kon Tiki, "Portland's Most Exotic Restaurant." Air France service to Tel Aviv, Hymie Shore's Kosher Meat Market, and Dave and Ralph Policar's Puritan Fish Market became regulars, along with Empire Chicken.

When Padrow resigned in 1961, the paper continued without an editor. It kept Portlanders up to date with a women's page, synagogue news and a column by high school student Trudi York. News from the Jewish Telegraphic Association and World News Service often filled half of the paper's eight pages. Stories focused on Israel ("UJA Campaign to help Romanians Emigrate to Israel") and anti-Semitism ("250,000 Moroccan Jews Suffer Hate Drive").

The 1967 Arab-Israeli War pushed everything aside. "As this issue of the Portland *Jewish Review* goes to press, the situation in the Middle East has reached a most critical stage," wrote JWFP president Hershal Tanzer. "I fervently hope that by the time you read this letter, tensions will have relaxed and the outlook for peace improved." The next issue, headlines blared "Portland Responds to Emergency—New Highs Reached in Giving."

By today's standards, some topics seemed absent and forgotten. Letters to the editor didn't appear until 1968. During the 1960s, the South Auditorium Urban Renewal Project leveled fifty-four blocks of the Jewish immigrant section of town. The newspaper didn't mention Urban Renewal. Only once did a boxed message announce: "Freeways Good or Bad, a free forum at the Jewish Community Center."

## *The* Review*'s Evolution*

Editor La Nita Anderson joined the paper in 1968 and stayed for eighteen years. Circulation expanded from Portland to statewide, and the paper was published monthly.

The *Review* featured local history. Shirley Nudelman, who grew up in South Portland, wrote a column titled "We Could Stroll Down Memory Lane but They Built a Freeway Over It." When the Jewish Community Center on Southwest Thirteenth Avenue closed with plans for a new location on Southwest Capitol Highway, a multipage story ran including photos of the Ramblers Memorial Bus and the 1926 Center Orchestra. The paper reflected Portlanders' concern about Soviet Jews. The 1972 Soviet Jewry rally in Portland made headlines, as did the September 1972 murder of Israeli athletes during the Munich Olympics.

Lydia Lipman talked about her time on the *Jewish Review* Board. "Anderson wanted the paper to be academic and philosophical," she said. "She wrote insightful articles about the rise of radical Islam. It was an early warning alert to what happened. Kudos to her."

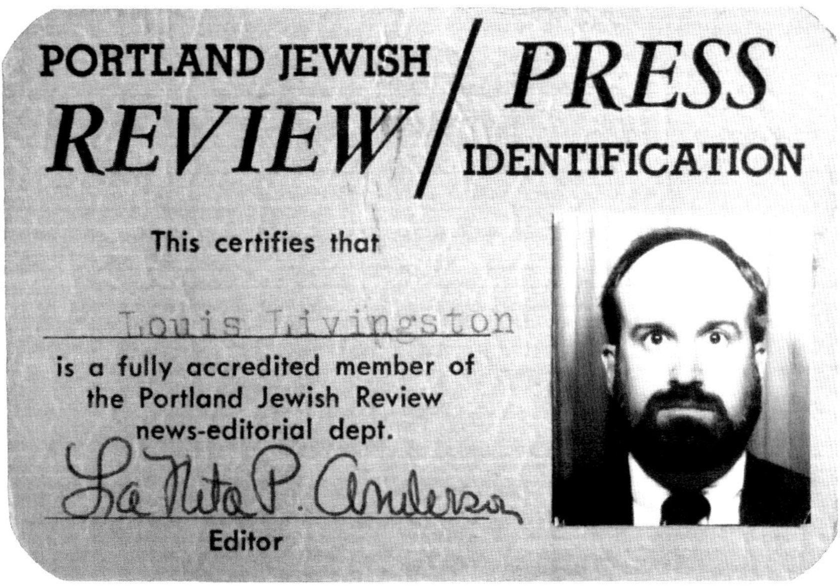


Louis Livingston used this *Jewish Review* press card for entry to the Cannes Film Festival. *Photo by author.*

Louis Livingston wrote book and movie reviews during Anderson's tenure. "I had a good time—and La Nita wanted reviews as often as possible," he said. "In one article, I compared *The Sorrow and the Pity* with the 1978 TV mini-series *Holocaust.*"

When Livingston left for a European summer holiday, he packed his press credential. "I remember going to the Cannes Film Festival," he said. "They said, 'Come on, nobody's heard of this newspaper,' but they relented and let me in. I interviewed an Israeli producer and wrote a long column."

Meanwhile, the paper's evolution continued. In 1973, JWFP adopted guidelines. The *Review*, it said, was "a combination house organ and newspaper that bases stories on a good news peg and deals with facts not opinion." A 1980 readership survey and other factors led to the 1984 headline, "34 Year Old Portland *Jewish Review* Begins New Era." Review

The *Jewish Review* front page on March 1967 included this photo and caption: "The Initial Gifts Dinner of the Jewish Welfare Federation of Portland held in March at the Benson Hotel, proved to be an outstanding event in the philanthropic history of our community. Hostesses for the Initial Gifts Dinner were: back row, from left: Mesdames Herbert Newmark, Martin Zell, Jerome Holzman, Hershal M. Tanzer, David W. Cohn, Harold H. Saltzman and Henry Blauer. Front row: Mesdames A. Victor Rosenfeld, Sol Director, and Gilbert Schnitzer." *Courtesy Ruth Saltzman/*Jewish Review.

Committee Chair and former editor Ben Padrow wrote, "The editorial policy of the new *Jewish Review* is contained within the masthead of the *New York Times*: to report the news impartially without fear or favor. The Oregon Jewish community may rely on this new community-owned *Jewish Review* to do two things: 1. To be a forum for the discussions of substantive ideas. 2. To be a catalyst for controversial ideas."

Anderson's article accompanied Padrow's: "In the past few years we ran features mostly by freelance writers on marriage counseling, the single parent, adoptions, keeping kosher, Russian Jewish newness, death or terminal illness, Jewish education, Hillel Academy's space problems, drug use, and Oregon prisons." She also noted stories on sin, religion, capital punishment, the arts and Israel/national news.

However, Anderson added, "What the Review has not had are enough letters to the editor to reflect the vitality of a community with strong opinions, nor articles written by those with differing points of view, particularly on local issues."

Help was on the way for this perceived omission—some thought too much so.

## *A Divided Jewish Agenda*

In 1985, Anderson retired from the *Jewish Review* and moved to her family home in La Grande. Elaine Cogan, a columnist for the *Oregonian* and *Oregon Journal*, stepped up as interim editor. "Not only will the Review be a communicator of news," she wrote in her first issue, "it also will be a forum for diverse opinion and commentary."

It started with a controversy that kept letters coming for years. When Chabad of Oregon wanted a Hanukah menorah in Pioneer Square, some did not approve. One *Review* had two pages of responses. The "No" view—signed by the American Jewish Committee, the Community Relations Committee, the Anti-Defamation league of B'nai B'rith and the Oregon Board of Rabbis—stated: "We strongly oppose the grant of a permit for the placement of any religious symbols in Pioneer Courthouse Square. We believe that issuance of such a permit would constitute violation of the federal and state constitutional principles requiring separation of church and state." Supporters argued that many cities displayed menorahs. Even President Jimmy Carter, they said, participated in the Washington, D.C., ceremony.

The next controversy drew attention outside the Jewish community. In March 1986, a founder of Jewish Americans for Middle East Understanding wrote an article under the headline "Palestinian-Israeli Relations Is Concern of Local Group." Controversial quotes included: "I believe that Israeli Jews and Palestinian Arabs can live peacefully side by side…I'm interested in learning more about the Arab-Israeli conflict. We love this land [Israel] and believe in its future…a union in common service of the land must be within the range of the possible."

Some agreed with the Portlander who responded in the next issue:

> *It is obvious that the Portland* Jewish Review *is totally under new editorship, and it no longer reflects the conservatism of this Jewish community…While it may well be stated that the paper should represent every facet of the community, this does not imply that those on the periphery should be given such strong recognition…I would hope that the Portland* Jewish Review *will be open to opinion from all sides, but seek to at least indicate that it represents the majority who are not amongst these nonobservant, bleary-eyed idealists.*

Controversy raged in subsequent letters. Even *Willamette Week* picked up the story in a June article titled "A Divided Jewish Agenda." It noted that while Portland's Jewish community was ten thousand strong, "small size by no means implies homogeneity." On the other hand, the paper reflected how readers united over the fate of Russian Jews, any serious threat to Israel and racism.

### *Paul Haist and Deborah Moon Join the* Review

Editor Paul Haist joined the paper in 1992. A native Portlander, Portland State University graduate and former *Oregonian*, *Oregon Journal* and *Seattle Post-Intelligencer* editor, he had spent the previous five years as a freelance writer and editor in Astoria. While the paper's appearance and tone became more professional, its interest in diverse opinions remained.

Rabbi Joshua Stampfer's article "Time Now for Compromise in the Middle East" produced a deluge of letters. He argued that Israeli security overshadowed "profound concerns about Jewish survival in America." To achieve peace, he wrote, "A compromise on the extent of land that Israel will continue to control in the West Bank and Gaza must be reached."

Other articles and letters reflected the community's opposition to Ballot Measure 9. Sponsored by the Oregon Citizens Alliance, the measure required government to discourage homosexuality.

One letter showed how times change and then change again. "Increasingly," the author wrote, "Jewish groups [in Portland] begin community events before Shabbat or Yom Tov are over. At dinners, non-kosher food is served without an option of food prepared according to kashrut. Money is handled on the Sabbath. Tradition deserves equal rights, too."

City Editor Deborah Moon joined the *Review* in December 1992. She had worked for a daily Colorado newspaper. Haist thanked the federation for committing the resources to make the hiring possible. "Our goal is to produce the kind of paper that wins the support and admiration—and the friendship—of the community it serves," he wrote.

*Jewish Review* city editor Deborah Moon, 2011. *Photo by author.*

That year, he clarified the paper's editorial position: "One simple truth about the Jewish community or any community is that it is likely to be home to more than one opinion on any given topic. In Oregon and Southwest Washington [the *Jewish Review*] has become one of the key forums for the exchange of ideas among Jews."

***

*JEWISH REVIEW* EDITORS

| | |
|---|---|
| 1959–61 | Ben Padrow |
| 1967 (two issues) | Elizabeth Till |
| September 1968–May 1985 | La Nita Anderson |
| June 1985–May 1987 | Elaine Cogan |
| September 1987–Summer 1989 | Marc Lowenthal |
| Summer 1989–January 1992 | Mara Woloshin |
| February 1, 1992–present | Paul Haist |

JEWISH NEWSPAPERS PUBLISHED IN PORTLAND

| | |
|---|---|
| 1893–1901 | *American Hebrew News* |
| 1903–1919 | *Jewish Tribune* |
| 1919–1953 | the *Scribe, A Record of Jewish Life and Thought* |
| 1959–present | the *Jewish Review* |

*JEWISH REVIEW* HONORS

Since the arrival of Haist and Moon at the *Jewish Review*, the paper has been honored numerous times for editorial excellence, including eight highly coveted Rockower Awards, presented annually by the American Jewish Press Association—four for Haist, three for Moon and one for occasional columnist Robert Horenstein.

The Oregon Newspaper Publishers Association and the Society for Professional Journalists have honored the paper and its writer-editors several times in recent years.

## Celebrating Twenty-five Years with Chabad

Browsing old *Jewish Review* editions sets the scene for Portland in 1984—like the article on Israel's thirty-sixth Independence Day or the ad for Policar's Passover specials. Then there was the Sunday program sponsored by the Mittleman Jewish Community Center "to find out what the future is in computers."

In February 1984, one article announced "New Family Arrives Here," with photos of Rabbi Moshe Wilhelm, his wife, Devorah, and children, Motti and Simi. They had just spent two years in Australia and came to Portland at the request of the New York Chabad Lubavitcher Rebbe Menachem Mendel Schneerson. "When Chabad comes into town," Wilhelm said in the article, "it tries to enhance existing organizations. Chabad works with the rabbis and the community to create new ideas."

Rabbi Moshe Wilhelm. *Courtesy Frank Barnett Photography.*

And over the past twenty-five years, Chabad of Oregon has enhanced thousands of lives through services, celebrations and education. As their silver anniversary approaches, we asked the Wilhelm family and friends to remember.

## *Coming to Oregon*

"We didn't know anyone," Wilhelm said about his family's 1984 arrival. They rented an apartment at the Shadow Hills complex on Vermont Street and turned one room into a combination office and shul.

"We schlepped in kosher food," Wilhelm said. "Fortunately, there were no excess baggage charges at that time." With no room to spare, they crammed the freezer into their bedroom and invited guests for Shabbos every week.

*Jewish Review* articles documented that first year's accomplishments, like the Purim kit for Russian immigrants, the twenty-four-hour Passover hotline and Seders complete with handmade matzah. Chabad visited hospitals and prisons and kept copies of its central text, the Tanya, available at its office.

By December, stories about a menorah controversy began and regularly appeared for years. While some Jewish leaders worried about separation of church and state, the Wilhelms celebrated lighting the menorah in the newly built Pioneer Courthouse Square. "Our hope is to reach not only people who come to shul," Wilhelm said. "Some are not ready to go to shul. We have to find ways to reach them in non-typical places."

Rabbi Motti Wilhelm, the eldest son, remembered those early times. "The manager of Shadow Hills helped us construct the first public menorah," he said. "It was made of PVC piping and spray painted." Young Wilhelm enjoyed visiting the Robison home and bringing presents of soup and challah. "I was my father's little helper. He used to tell [the residents] stories in Yiddish, and I'd sit alongside."

The addition of Albertson's kosher section remains a family standout. "They brought in Riesman's Cake," Motti Wilhelm said. "It was a small brownie in the freezer section. It was such a thrill to buy kosher food there."

He also remembered his family parking a flatbed truck with a sukkah in downtown Portland, a project that continues today. "We ask people if they've heard the shofar or would like the opportunity." In one 1984 article, Moshe Wilhelm called the lack of Jewish education—"Genuine Torah, as it was handed down to us three and a half thousand years ago"—the most pressing issue in the Oregon Jewish community.

The couple started the Aleph Bais School, the Bar Mitzvah College Tutorial Program and weekly senior citizen classes. With help from Seattle students, they developed a free ten-day Yeshiva experience, with sessions ranging from Jewish mysticism to the synagogue service. In 1985, the Wilhelms offered their second season of Gan Israel Kiddycamp at the "spacious Shadow Hills Complex."

## *Moving to Scholls Ferry Road*

By 1988, the family were living in their Hillsdale home and had moved Congregation Bais Menachem, their school and their office to Scholls Ferry Road in Beaverton.

"Around the school were all trees and deer signs," said Vicki Stone, who has been active with Chabad for twenty years. "It was rural. The school was an old house next door to a quarry. If you looked out the back, you'd see a downward slope to this lake where we would toivel our dishes. Every Friday, the Wilhelms hosted a big dinner. Then they'd set up cots, and anyone who needed to slept over." They held services the next day.

The school grew, the Wilhelm family grew and traffic to Beaverton grew. By 1998, they had relocated to the present site of Maimonides Jewish Day School on Southwest Vermont Street. (The preschool is still called Aleph Bet.)

Kathy Pearson of Portland remembers attending shul in the converted garage. "If it were nice weather, they'd get a tent over the patio and have services out there," she said. "One year it was raining, and the wind blew the tent. This big flood of water came down on the women's section."

"The shul was like a shtibl," said longtime friend Lee Rosenstock, referring to the small rooms where Hasidic Jews combined prayer, study and a social center. "One member was a great Sephardic cook. She prepared a huge pan of cholent for after services on Saturday. Everyone stayed."

Today, Chabad's Portland office is located in the same building as the Jewish Federation of Greater Portland. While Moshe Wilhelm once traveled throughout Oregon, Chabad now has centers in Ashland, Bend, Eugene, Hillsboro and southwest Washington. Portland campus emissaries Rabbi Dov and Chani Bialo welcome students to their home each week.

The Jewish Learning Institute, directed by Motti Wilhelm, offers classes throughout the year.

In April 2008, the *Jewish Review* reported that the JFGP's umbrella had expanded to include Maimonides Jewish Day School. And Moshe Wilhelm recently announced plans for a new campus across from the school. "It will be the nerve center for all the activities Chabad does," he said. "That's going to be our Chabad Center for Portland—and, for that matter, for the whole state of Oregon."

*Author's Note: Chabad Oregon moved to its new center in 2009. Today, there are nine regional centers and ten full-time rabbis. Rabbi Moshe Wilhelm focuses on outreach, development and Chabad's continued expansion. Rabbi Motti Wilhelm has assumed leadership of Congregation Bais Menachem.*

## WHITE ARYAN RESISTANCE CASE GALVANIZED THE COMMUNITY

On November 13, 1988, three racist skinheads tried to drive past a parked car on a narrow street in Southeast Portland. The fight that broke out left one of the car's Ethiopian occupants dead.

Mulugeta Seraw was beaten over the head with a baseball bat so hard that the bat broke in two. According to a *New York Times* report, his killer, Ken Mieske, said that he and the others killed him "because of his race." Mieske was convicted of first-degree murder. Fellow East Side White Pride members Kyle Brewster and Steve Strasser were convicted of manslaughter and assault.

Meanwhile, in California, White Aryan Resistance (WAR) leader Tom Metzger praised the trio for performing their "civic duty." He had sent a young protégé named Dave Mazella to Portland to recruit and preach for the cause. Mazella was in town during the murder, but back in California he had an apparent change of heart. According to *A Hundred Little Hitlers*, by Elinor Langer, he called the Anti-Defamation League (ADL) in Santa Ana and explained that he wanted to leave the Aryan Youth Movement. The ADL contacted Morris Dees at the Southern Poverty Law Center (SPLC). Mazella agreed to testify against Metzger.

The SPLC and ADL financed the wrongful death civil lawsuit, officially called *Berhanu v. Metzger* but better known as the White Aryan Resistance/ Skinheads case. Like other lawsuits of its kind, the intention was to award money to the survivors of the person who was killed as a result of negligence or intentional acts. The attorneys asserted that Tom Metzger and his son, John, were responsible for the murder. The jury agreed and awarded Seraw's family $12.5 million in damages.

Morris Dees of the SPLC provided lead counsel. Portland attorney Elden Rosenthal provided local counsel for the ADL. He got involved when an ADL organizer invited Portland civil rights lawyers to dinner with Morris Dees.

"Morris asked if anyone would like to be co-counsel on a pro bono basis," Rosenthal said. "I remember saying, 'I've waited my entire career for this case.' Many members of my family died during the Holocaust, so it was emotionally satisfying to do this case against a neo-Nazi."

Rosenthal doesn't recall an initial reaction to Tom Metzger. "He was just an ordinary-looking guy with a bad toupee," he said. "We had a wonderful jury consultant. I had little concern. Whether you were black or white, if you lived in Portland you wouldn't like this."

Attorney Elden Rosenthal worked with Morris Dees of the Southern Poverty Law Center for eighteen months preparing the wrongful death suit against white supremacist Tom Metzger. *Photo by author.*

It was a strong case, Rosenthal said, "extremely dramatic. Mazella testified that Metzger instructed him to come to Portland and recruit skinheads. Metzger took the witness stand in his own defense. He wanted the publicity. When he got on the stand, he asked himself questions from a script he'd worked out."

Memories include twenty-four-hour police protection. "Morris was security conscious because there were attempts on his life," Rosenthal said. "In the run-up to the trial, there was a bomb placed on the courthouse steps with a note relating to our case. I received a couple of anonymous death threats, but it didn't seem serious to me. It seemed serious to the Portland police."

"The most vivid memories I have from the trial didn't occur in the courtroom," he continued. "My rabbi got married, and I went to the wedding with police protection. There were two reception lines. One was for Joey and Lisa, and the other was to talk to me and thank me. It galvanized the community in a way I hadn't seen."

Portland State sociology professor Randy Blazak directs the Hate Crimes Research Network. Originally from Stone Mountain, Georgia, the second birthplace of the Ku Klux Klan, he was studying skinheads in Orlando, Florida, at the time of Seraw's murder. Although things change quickly, he's kept rough track of those involved. Ken Mieske, he said, remains at the Oregon State Penitentiary.

"Kyle Brewster was paroled but is still involved with racist skinheads and has gone back to prison a few times," Blazak said. "Steve Strasser was released and has left the movement. Dave Mazella became a born-again Christian and may have a ministry in California. He became a spokesperson against racism. John Metzger hasn't popped up on the radar. Tom Metzger is still in the movement."

Tom Metzger lives in Warsaw, Indiana. His website (www.resist.com/radio.htm) explains his philosophy: "The Insurgent is a network of highly motivated White Racists. Each person is an individual in his or her own right. The insurgent promotes the Lone Wolf tactical concept. Made up of individuals and small cells."

Blazak, Rosenthal and most others agree that Metzger is discredited among his peers. "We collected money from Metzger until we couldn't," Rosenthal said. "There's a limit. You can only collect money on a judgment for twenty years." Money from the settlement went to Mulugeta Seraw's son. A SPLC lawyer involved in the case adopted and raised him in America. He returned to Ethiopia and became a pilot for Ethiopian airlines.

"The case had two purposes," Rosenthal said.

> *The first was to bankrupt Metzger and the White Aryan Resistance, and the second was public education. Did it have desired affect? Certainly in the short run. There was a lot of public outrage over Metzger and what he stood for. My view is, there's a certain irreducible number of people who are going to be right-wing neo-Nazi types. You will never rid them from a free society. Every generation needs to educate their children about the danger these people pose. To me, that was the value of the case.*

## NCJW Archives Chapter History

When the Portland Section of the National Council of Jewish Women started in 1896, the founders saw change coming.

Since 1849, the city's German Jews had settled, prospered and built beautiful homes in Nob Hill. Now Eastern European and Sephardic Jews flooded South Portland, many of them poor, with few skills and little secular education. Soon, the NCJW founded the Neighborhood House and offered citizenship classes, a medical clinic and athletics among the many programs. A long line of projects that helped Portland's Jewish and non-Jewish community followed.

By the time the NCJW sold the Neighborhood House in 2001, records of those early years lay in a storage facility, hidden from the public and in disarray. Former president Rose Rustin decided to act. She contacted three NCJW leaders and Oregon Jewish Museum curator Anne LeVant Prahl. In 2005, the NCJW archive project began with the goal of donating the collection to OJM. Today, Rustin, Carol Chestler, Shirley Rackner and Sharon Tarlow have almost completed their mission.

"We were all coughing and sneezing," said Rackner about their first visit to the NCJW storage facility. "It was overwhelming." They saw dozens of the *Neighborhood Cookbook*s published in 1914 and 1932 and a huge box of roller skates. They found ledger books, membership lists and articles of

Sharon Tarlow (far left), Carol Chestler, Shirley Rackner and Rose Rustin organize the archives of the National Council of Jewish Women at the Oregon Jewish Museum. *Photo by author.*

incorporation, along with handwritten books with memos, like one about Mrs. Bloom donating twenty-five cents. "The minutes and budgets were the most fun—just the handwriting, the gorgeous script," Rackner said.

Early settlement work records revealed poverty. "Many sad things motivated the NCJW to support the immigrants with daycare, juvenile justice and hospital beds at St. Vincents," Rustin said. "We have files on the organizations that met [at the Neighborhood House] and the dispensary files."

They found World War II–era appeals from displaced persons searching for family and from organizations relocating European Jews. They found dance programs and photos from the Angel Ball. "We wore long gowns," Tarlow said about these fundraisers for the Council Thrift Shop, a downtown charity that ran from 1964 until 2007. "We call them costumes now. They're probably in some vintage store or on the backs of twentysomethings."

After a year spent emptying the storage facility, the women brought things deemed worthy of archiving to Rackner's basement. Here they sorted for another two years. Finally, fourteen boxes went to OJM, where work continued.

Looking back, the archivists find their interest easy to explain. "We are all past NCJW leaders," Chestler said. "This organization is where we grew up, where we learned how to be administrators. It was a steppingstone for our careers, and we didn't want the history discarded."

"I was most fascinated by what the early women did," Rustin said. "They raised so much money for their time."

"Remembering all the things we did and others before us was motivating," said Rackner. "And what an impact the organization made. It gave us a sense of our own mortality. We were there. NCJW was there. We are part of a parade of people who have carried out projects to make the community a better place."

## Seniors Clap Hands to Yoga

She asked the residents to nestle into their seats before she moved on to breathing and movement. "Start with knowing what's underneath you," she said. "Another wriggle, another snuggle, and we'll just get going."

Louise Lorente (standing center, background) leads seniors in a yoga class at the Adult Day Care program at Robison Jewish Health Center at Cedar Sinai Park. *Photo by author.*

Louise Lorente's yoga classes at the Robison Jewish Health Center and Adult Day Care have been going for almost three years. Tailor-made for the elderly, including those with Alzheimer's disease, she emphasizes stretching, relaxation and, most of all, laughter.

"There aren't enough opportunities for movement throughout the day," said activity coordinator Patti Garland. I'm amazed how much movement Louise gets and how much they try." Garland doesn't tell residents that they're going to an exercise class. "The key to getting people to come is telling them it's laughing-yoga."

Lorente began by prompting the group. "Let's start with a soft laugh," she said. "Inhale deeply, and laugh quietly."

Everyone clapped their hands rhythmically and whispered, "Ha, Ha, Ho Ho, Ho." The next try was louder. Finally they came to what Lorente called bring-the-house-down laughter. By that time, everyone was smiling.

To Lorente, teaching yoga is always new and fresh. The former Portland Public School English as a Second Language teacher became seriously involved with yoga while fighting fibromyalgia and chronic pain ten years ago. "They gave me every medicine," she said. "It didn't help, and yoga did." Now she gets her inspiration from the people in the room. "This is not a DVD with a script."

"Inhale and one arm up, spread your fingers out," she continued. "Exhale, fingers come together. Very good."

"I haven't done exercise like this for a long time, and I'm having pain. Should I stop?" asked a new Robison resident.

"That's a good question. There should be no pain," Lorente answered. "And if you can't move a body part, here's a trick: just imagine that it's moving."

## *Yoga for Seniors*

The benefits of yoga are anything but imaginary, according to OHSU clinical psychologist Jim Carson. He and his wife, Kimberly, tested their Yoga of Awareness program at Duke University research trials. "We demonstrated improvements in mood, fatigue and pain," he said.

"I've seen huge benefits with senior citizens and yoga," said Kimberly Carson, who has a master's in public health and is a registered yoga teacher. She taught in retirement centers for many years. "One woman in her early eighties had osteoarthritis such that her feet were almost clubbed. In three weeks of yoga practice, she was able to stand up in a steady way without her walker."

While that was a dramatic example, Kimberly Carson often sees increased flexibility and strength, as well as decreased insomnia. "General life functioning is improved with yoga," she said.

"It's important that it be a gentle approach to yoga if it's for seniors," Jim Carson cautioned. "You want to have a teacher that is competent in working with seniors, but you also want to use your own judgment."

## *Using a Gentle Approach*

At Cedar Sinai Park, Lorente's gentle approach begins with greeting each resident by name and continues with encouragement:

"Press into this foot and lift your other foot. Very good, Bertha. Wow!"

"Mary Betty, you're laughing and smiling already."

As is her custom, Lorente stopped the class a few times to tell a joke, warning people that they might moan. "What did the big chimney say to the little chimney?" she asked. The punch line: "You're too young to smoke."

"Exhale and bring your arms into Namaste," Lorente said. She ends each class with a kundalini yoga farewell blessing:

*May the long time sun*
*Shine upon you,*
*All love surround you,*
*And the pure light within you*
*Guide your way on.*

"Namaste," Lorente said as she stood and gave everyone a goodbye hug or handshake.

"What does Namaste mean?" someone asked.

"It means, 'I see the beauty in you,'" Lorente said, "and, 'I honor you.'"

# MAH JONGG: THE TILES THAT BIND

"Mah Jongg in Florida is different," Dorothy Dworkin explained above the sound of clicking tiles. "Not brutal, but they do take it seriously."

"That's just her group's table rules," said another, referring to the adjustments all players make so that regulations fit their style. And, therein lies the saying: the Chinese took one thousand years to develop one way to play Mah Jongg; the Jews took one year to develop one thousand ways.

And Mah Jongg keeps on developing at Neveh Shalom every Monday from 1:00 p.m. to 4:00 p.m. "It's been ongoing for about ten years," said Ann Kruss, the group's founder and former instructor. She started by teaching Mah Jongg at the Mittleman Jewish Community Center, and the group has met since. "We have a different number every week and adjust our tables accordingly."

Mah Jongg started in China, but nobody knows when. American interest began with Charles Babcock, a Standard Oil representative, in Soo Chow.

Playing Mah Jongg requires a balance between the serious and the not-too-serious, according to some of the players who frequent the Monday Mah Jongg games at Congregation Neveh Shalom. *Front table, from left, clockwise*: Carol Jaffee, Dorothy Dworkin, Leatrice Kaplan and Bryna Montgomery. Ann Kruss, the founder of the weekly game, is at top left. *Photo by author.*

He brought the first sets to the United States in 1920, and within two years the game had taken off.

The documentary *The Tiles that Bind* explores Mah Jongg's popularity with Jewish women. The proximity of tenement life, most women staying home during the day and the passage of tradition from mother to daughter—all are possible explanations.

"I have no idea why Jewish women like this game so much," said Linda Kline, who was in Portland for the summer. Linda came home from school every day to her mother's clicking tiles and "swore I'd never play this game." Still, when Kline moved to a new community, it provided a way to meet people. "Now, I really like it," she said. "It's reminiscent of our youth, watching our mothers play, but it's also a common ground for women to get together."

Today, twelve women gathered at three tables—four players per game. Everyone concentrated. Calling out the suit of discarded tiles provided background to occasional conversation:

"Grand Central has the best Challah."

"They brought kosher meat all the way from Chicago."

"I played Mah Jongg one place you couldn't talk or anything."

"That's silly; it's a game."

Each woman kept a small purse next to her tiles. "The most you lose in one day is two dollars," said Leatrice Kaplan.

Watching one another's moves carefully, the women tried to guess their opponent's hand.

"Some bridge players actually look down on Mah Jongg," Kaplan continued. "I maintain that if you play defensively, it takes just as much brain power as bridge."

So what makes someone good at Mah Jongg?

"Someone who knows how to laugh," said one player.

"Someone who knows when to be quiet," said another.

"It's a balance between serious and not too serious," said a woman who has played for forty-five years.

"You play to win," said another as she shifted tiles on her rack. "You play to win," she said again.

*Appendix I*

# Map of Old South Portland

*This map shows the approximate original location of places mentioned in the book. The northern South Portland boundary was roughly Southwest Hall Street (24).*

Key

| | |
|---|---|
| 1 | Gevurtz Hall |
| 2 | Wintler's Drugstore |
| 3 | Manley Community Center* |
| 4 | Failing School after 1913* |
| 5 | Jewish Shelter Home before 1935* |
| 6 | Leo Greenstein's home |
| 7 | Neighborhood House* |
| 8 | Nurse's Residence* |
| 9 | Lair Hill Park* |
| 10 | South Portland Library* |
| 11 | Gussie Kirshner Reinhardt's home and barn |
| 12 | Kesser Israel Synagogue* |
| 13 | Duniway Park * |
| 14 | Portland Kosher Meat Market |
| 15 | Calistro and Halperin's Delicatessen |
| 16 | Mosler's Bakery |

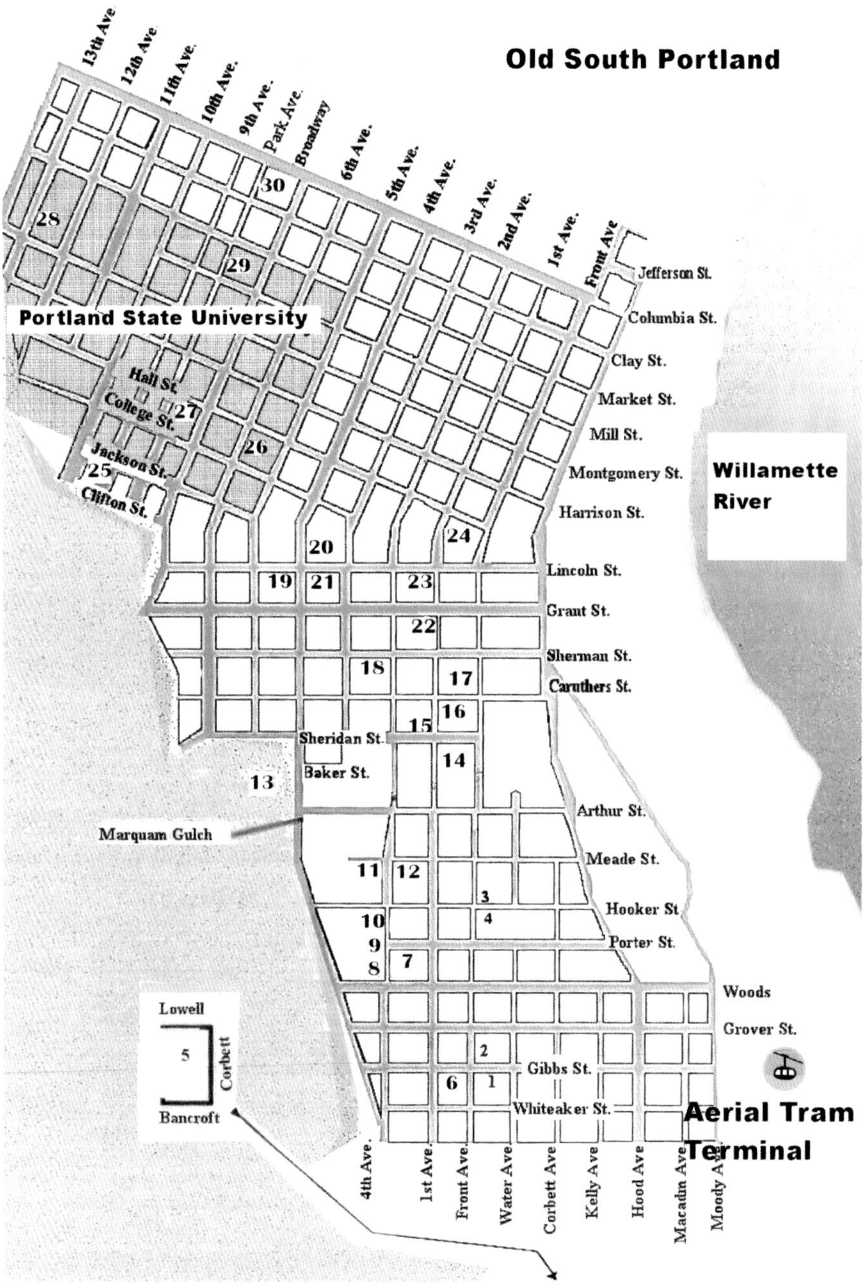


This map shows the approximate locations of places mentioned in the book. The northern boundary of South Portland was located at about Southwest Hall Street. *Map by author, with background grid derived from Steven Lowenstein's* The Jews of Oregon, *page 102.*

17 Mrs. Levine's Fish Market
18 Ahavath Achim Synagogue
19 Jerry Stern's home
20 Fourth Street Garage
21 Lincoln Theater
22 First Avenue (Grant Street) Theater
23 Portland Kosher Meat Market
24 Shaarie Torah Synagogue
25 Frieda Cohen's home
26 Neveh Tzedek Talmud Torah
27 Shattuck School*
28 B'nai B'rith Building
29 Lincoln High (1912–1952)*
30 Temple Ahavai Shalom

* Indicates that the structure is still standing.

*Appendix II*

# Portland Population Statistics

The dates and statistics in this table are approximate.

| Year | Portland Population | Portland Jewish Population |
|---|---|---|
| 1860 | 2,874[1] | 120[4] |
| 1870 | 8,293[1] | 429[4] |
| 1880 | 17,577[1] | 490[4] |
| 1890 | 46,385[1] | unknown |
| 1900 | 90,426[1] | 1,900[5] |
| 1910 | 207,214[1] | unknown |
| 1920 | 275,000[1] | 9,000[7] |
| 1930 | 299,122[1] | 11,000[1] |
| 1946 | unknown | 7,128[6] |
| 1960 | 372,676[3, 9] | 7,832 (1957)[6, 9] |
| 1970 | 379,967[3] | 8,000 (1968)[1] |
| 1980 | 366,383[3] | 8,735[1] |
| 1990 | 437,319[8] | 9,000[1] |
| 2000 | 529,121[2] | 25,000[1] |
| 2010 | 583,776[2] | 45,700[6] |

## Notes

1. *American Jewish Yearbook*. American Jewish Committee Archives. www.ajcarchives.org.

2. "Certified Population Estimates for Oregon and Oregon Counties." Portland State University. www.pdx.edu/sites/www.pdx.edu.prc/files/media_assets/2010_PL94_cities_M-P.pdf.

3. Census of Population and Housing, 1980 Census, Oregon, chapter A, 1980a_orABC-01.pdf, Table 5, Population of Places: 1960–1980. www.census.gov/prod/www/abs/decennial/1980cenpopv1.html.

4. Toll, William. *The Making of an Ethnic Middle Class.* New York: State University of New York Press, 1982.

5. Toll, William. "Fraternalism and Community Structure on the Urban Frontier: The Jews of Portland, Oregon, a Case Study." *Pacific Historical Review* 47, no. 3 (August 1978).

6. Jewish Welfare Federation of Portland/Jewish Federation of Greater Portland.

7. The AJC 1920–21 yearbook listed the population as 2,500 but noted "9000 according to a recent estimate of the Federation of Jewish Charities of that city."

8. Federation for American Immigration Reform. "City Factsheet: Portland, Oregon." www.fairus.org/site/PageNavigator/facts/city_data_or_portland.

9. The Jewish Welfare Federation of Portland's 1957 Jewish census included Vancouver, Washington, most of Multnomah County and parts of Clackamas and Washington Counties. According to the survey, the total population of this area was 570,000, out of which 7,832 were Jews.

*Appendix III*

# GLOSSARY

**bima**: an elevated area in the Jewish synagogue on which stands the person reading the Torah aloud.

**"Bintel Brief"**: an advice column in the *Jewish Daily Forward*.

**cheder**: Jewish religious school for elementary school students.

**kashrut**: Jewish dietary laws.

**kehila**: a community.

**latkes**: potato pancakes.

**pishka**: a collection box.

**Sephardic**: descendants of Jews from the Iberian Peninsula.

**shochet**: an authorized kosher butcher.

**shofar**: a horn used for Jewish religious rituals.

**shtetl**: a small village in Eastern Europe.

**shtibl**: small rooms where Hasidic Jews combined prayer, study and a social center.

**shul**: a synagogue.

**sukkah**: a temporary dwelling used during the holiday of Sukkot.

**Talmud Torah**: a school at which children are instructed in Judaism.

**toival**: a ritual of making utensils and dishes kosher.

**yeshiva**: a seminary.

**Yiddish**: a language derived mainly from German and Hebrew and spoken by Jews from Central and Eastern Europe.

# Bibliography

## Books

Atwood, Kay. *Illahe: The Story of Settlement in the Rogue River Canyon.* Corvallis: Oregon State University Press, 2002.

Clough, Bess. *One Hundred Years in Canyonville, 1858–1958: Then and Now.* Canyonville, OR: Douglas Fir Printing Co, 1958.

Gaston, Joseph. *Portland, Oregon: Its History and Builders.* Chicago, IL: S.J. Clarke Publishing Company, 1911.

Goeres-Gardner, Diane L. *Necktie Parties: Legal Executions in Oregon 1851–1905.* Caldwell, ID: Caxton Press, 1995.

Langor, Elinor. *A Hundred Little Hitlers.* New York: Metropolitan Books, 2003.

Lee, Samuel J. *Moses of the New World: The Work of Baron de Hirsch.* New York: Thomas Yoseloff, 1970.

Lowenstein, Steven. *The Jews of Oregon 1850–1950.* Portland: Jewish Historical Society of Oregon, 1987.

McCarthy, Linda. *A History of Oregon Sheriffs.* Salem: Oregon Sheriffs Association, 1992.

Miranda, Gary. *Following a River: Portland's Congregation Neveh Shalom 1869–1989*. Portland, OR: Congregation Neveh Shalom, 1989.

Nodel, Rabbi Julius. *The Ties Between: A Century of Judaism on America's Last Frontier*. Portland, OR: Temple Beth Israel, 1959.

Rockaway, Robert A. *Words of the Uprooted: Jewish Immigrants in Early Twentieth-Century America*. Ithaca, NY: Cornell University Press, 1998.

Toll, William. *The Making of an Ethnic Middle Class*. New York: State University of New York Press, 1982.

## JOURNALS

Clark, Dr. Dan E. "Traditions of the Summer Session." *Old Oregon* (April 1927): 15. University of Oregon.

Dakers, Hazel. "Norden & Mansfield Families of Portland, Oregon." *Shalshelet, a Publication of the Jewish Genealogical Society of Oregon* (Summer 2008).

Jensen, Kimberly. "Neither Head nor Tail to the Campaign." *Oregon History Quarterly* 108, no. 3.

Toll, William. "Ethnicity and Stability: The Italians and Jews of South Portland, 1900–1940." *Pacific Historical Review* 54 (May 1985).

———. "Fraternalism and Community Structure on the Urban Frontier." *Pacific Historical Review* 47, no. 3 (August 1978): 369–403.

## Newspaper Articles

*American Hebrew News*, 1893–1901, Oregon Historical Society Research Library, Portland Oregon.

Calvert, Shotwell. "Refugees in City." *Oregonian*, December 25, 1938.

Edwards, Herman. "Ja, We Are Happy." *Oregonian*, April 16, 1939.

*Jewish Review.* "New JEA President Is Harold Schnitzer." May 1964.

———. "Portland Responds to Emergency." September 1967.

———. "Portland to Welcome New Family." November 1964.

———. "Refugees Start New Life in Community." June 1988.

*Jewish Tribune.* "Jewish Colony Thrives: Experiment in Oregon Said to Be Marked Success, Band Located Near Bend Prospers First Year According to Report and Others Are Expected." June 21, 1913.

———. "Jews as Farmers: Officials Visiting Portland Aid Five Thousand Families." July 28, 1911.

———. "Leave for Farm Colony: Forward to Soil Is Slogan of Party Who Left Sunday." September 6, 1912.

———. "Portland Zionist Society Organized." June 21, 1912.

———. "To Aid Jewish Farmers." July 5, 1912.

———. "25 Jewish Families Off For Central Oregon." August 30, 1912.

———. "Woman's Suffrage." March 29, 1912.

———. "Woman Suffrage." May 24, 1912.

*Lake County Examiner.* "Colonization in Northern Lake: Advance Party File on Five 320-Acre Homesteads on Railroad Survey." October 3, 1912.

———. "Jewish Colony Is Successful: Settlement in Eastern Oregon Shows What May Be Done." July 3, 1913.

*Morning Oregonian.* "Annual ICOR Ball Set for March 7." March 1, 1936.

———. "Chest Plans Drafted: Charitable Institutions of City at Meeting." November 23, 1920.

———. "Community Chest Close-Ups: Intimate Glimpses of Portland Welfare Workers." September 30, 1931.

———. "The Courts. Object of the Assessment." December 9, 1885.

———. "Early Cemeteries, Places of Sepulture Now in the Heart of the City." April 26, 1887.

———. "ICOR Meeting Booked." May 2, 1934.

———. "ICOR Picnic Sunday." July 27, 1934.

———. "In Sparta, Union County." February 4, 1873.

———. "Jewish Bodies Get Aid: 11 Organizations to Participate in Community Chest Fund." February 25, 1921.

———. "Jewish Drive Planned: $50,000 to Be Raised for Relief and Social Service Budget." January 4, 1920.

———. "Jewry Hastens Welfare Drive: National Leaders Picture Chaos After Olympic Games." April 1, 1936.

———. "Junk Men Get Charter: Gevurtz Hall Jammed Full with Jubilant Celebrants." October 12, 1928.

———. “Machinery on Exhibit.” February 8, 1934.

———. “Marquam Gulch to Be Used as Dumping Place for Garbage.” May 30, 1914.

———. “Park Plan Favored, Citizens in Other Parts Give Way to South Portland.” September 24, 1916, Section 1.

———. “Relief Funds Planned: Repeated Solicitations to Be Eliminated: Ben Selling and Julius L. Meier Head Committee Named to Raise Money.” September 17, 1927.

———. “Southern Oregon: Recent Development Have Proven Very Satisfactory, a Dual Formation of Gold and Silver Extends from the Rogue River to the Clackamas,” June 1, 1889.

———. “A Trip through Josephine County.” February 15, 1865.

*New York Times.* “Guilt Admitted in Racial Killing.” May 3, 1989. www.nytimes.com/1989/05/03/us/guilt-admitted-in-racial-killing.html.

*North Powder News.* “Herman Rothchild Buried in Portland: Pioneer Merchant Laid to Rest in Beth Israel Cemetery.” November 15, 1924.

*Oregonian.* “Open House Planned.” March 14, 1943.

———. “Refugees from China Tell of Hardships.” October 16, 1948.

———. “Service Men to Be Guests.” November 14, 1943.

———. “Welfare Group Names Cabinet.” November 10, 1956.

Rein, Moses. “Kosher Riot and Woman Suffrage.” *Jewish Tribune*, February 23, 1912.

*Scribe.* “American Jewry to Be Asked to Raise $10,000,000 to Finance Emigration of German Jews During 1936.” February 7, 1936.

———. "Annual Report of the Federated Jewish Societies." January 21, 1921.

———. "Federation–Welfare Fund Merger." June 1952.

———. "ICOR Meeting to Feature Movie of Biro-Bidjan." October 7, 1938.

———. "Jewish Community Center Organized to Take Over B'nai B'rith Center." August 19, 1938.

———. "Portland Jewry Prepares for Welfare Campaign." March 13, 1936.

———. "Portland to Consider Advisability of Creating a Fund for Relief of Non-Local Charities." January 7, 1927.

———. "Thousands of Jews Flee Polish City After Pogrom." June 12, 1936.

———. "Union of Portland Jewish Social Agencies." October 10, 1919.

Sills, Tom. "ADL Defends Plaintiffs at Metzger Trial." *Jewish Review*, October 17, 1990.

*Weekly Oregonian.* "Contributions to the U.S. Sanitary Commission Fund." October 11, 1862.

———. Letter from Congregation Beth Israel's Secretary Ben Norden. August 24, 1861.

*Willamette Week.* "A Divided Jewish Agenda." June 5, 1986.

## PAMPHLETS AND THESIS

Bureau of Land Management. *Rogue River Ranch.* Oregon-Medford District Office, August 2004. www.blm.gov.

Levison, Robert. "The Jews of Jacksonville." Master's thesis, University of Oregon, 1962.

Lifshitz, Tanya. *In the Beginning: An English-Russian Guidebook for New Immigrants.* Portland, OR: Jewish Family and Child Service, 1981.

## Manuscripts and Archival Materials

Albany City Directory, 1878. Mansfield & Monteith, Publishers. Albany Regional Museum, Albany, Oregon.

All Civil War Pension Index, General Index to Pension File (Julius Joseph), 1861–1934. www.ancestry.com.

*American Jewish Yearbook.* American Jewish Committee Archives. www.ajcarchives.org.

Digital Archive of Historic Photographs. Baker County Library, Oregon. http://68.178.234.42/webphoto.

Federated Jewish Societies of Portland Annual Report, 1927. Multnomah County Library, Portland, Oregon.

Hebrew Agricultural Association of Oregon. Certificate of Filing and Recording Articles of Incorporation: File no. 17335, Oregon State Archives, Salem, Oregon.

Industrial Removal Office Records, 1899–1922. American Jewish Historical Society, Newton Center, Massachusetts, and New York. http://www.cjh.org/p/61.

Jacob Fleischner Donation Land Claim. Oregon Genealogical Society, Portland, Oregon.

Jewish burial records. http://userdb.rootsweb.ancestry.com/cemeteries.

Jewish Census, Portland Urbanized Area. Jewish Federation of Portland, October 1957.

Mayers, Jacob. Record of Patents: Patent No. 533639, Lakeview 06082. Bureau of Land Management, Portland, Oregon.

Minute Book of the First Hebrew Congregation of Albany, Oregon, 1878–1924. Oregon Historical Society Research Library, Portland, Oregon.

Office of the City Auditor. Portland City Archives, photographs. http://efiles.ci.portland.or.us.

Oregon Jewish Museum. "Gladys Trachtenberg Oral History," December 11, 1973. Portland, Oregon.

Oregon Suffrage Associations. National American Woman Suffrage Association records, Library of Congress.

Pacific Coast Directory, 1867. www.ancestry.com.

Pearlman, David. Record of Patents: Patent Number 769946, Lakeview 09136. Bureau of Land Management, Portland, Oregon.

Polk's Portland City Directories. Multnomah County Library, Portland, Oregon.

Principals of social work class list, summer session, 1912. University of Oregon Archives. Courtesy of Dr. Nancy Korloff.

State Historic Preservation League (SHPO), Salem. http://heritagedata.prd.state.or.us/historic.

U.S. Federal Census Collection. www.ancestry.com.

*William G. Obenauer's 1892 Classified Business Directory.* Albany, Oregon. Genealogy Trails. www.genealogytrails.com/ore/linn/census/directories/1892_albanybiz.html.

# Index

## T



## U



## V



## W



## Y



## Z

# About the Author

Polina Olsen writes a "Looking Back" column for the *Jewish Review* newspaper and contributes to several local and national publications. Her three previous books, *A Walking Tour of Historic Jewish Portland*, *The Immigrants' Children, Jewish and Italian Memories of Old South Portland* and *The Downtown Jews: A Walking Tour through Portland's Early Business District*, have been well received. She also leads walking tours of the historic Jewish and Italian immigrant district during the summer months.

Mrs. Olsen grew up in New York and moved to Oregon in 1977. She is a University of Oregon graduate in computer science and worked for high technology companies for more than twenty years. She traveled throughout Asia and South America for several years and lived in England with her British husband, Andy.

Polina Olsen lives in Portland with Andy and cats Baba Ghanoush and Koshka.